GO

BACK

AND

FETCH

IT

GO BACK AND FETCH IT

RECOVERING EARLY BLACK MUSIC IN THE AMERICAS FOR FIDDLE AND BANJO

Kristina R. Gaddy and Rhiannon Giddens

The University of North Carolina Press
CHAPEL HILL

This book was published with the assistance
of the William R. Kenan Jr. Fund of the
University of North Carolina Press.

Manufactured in the United States of America

Designed and typeset by Lindsay Starr in Latienne Pro and Rosella

Cover art: violin © Adobe Stock/KseniaKrop; banjo in Sloane, *Voyage to the Islands*;
rhythmic patterns in Focke, *West-Indië*

LIBRARY OF CONGRESS CATALOGING-IN-PUBLICATION DATA

Names: Gaddy, Kristina R. author | Giddens, Rhiannon, 1977- author

Title: Go back and fetch it : recovering early Black music in the Americas
for fiddle and banjo / Kristina R. Gaddy and Rhiannon Giddens.

Description: Chapel Hill : The University of North Carolina Press, 2025. |
Includes bibliographical references and index.

Identifiers: LCCN 2025013891 | ISBN 9781469690575 paperback alk. paper |
ISBN 9781469683096 epub | ISBN 9781469690582 pdf

Subjects: LCSH: African Americans—Music—19th century—History and criticism |
African Americans—Music—18th century—History and criticism | Black people—
America—Music—19th century—History and criticism | Black people—America—
Music—18th century—History and criticism | African Americans—Music | Black
people—America—Music | Folk music—United States | Folk music—America |
Violin music—Scores | Banjo music—Scores | BISAC: MUSIC / Ethnomusicology |
HISTORY / World | LCGFT: Folk songs | Scores | Songbooks

Classification: LCC ML3556 .G24 2025 | DDC 780.89/96—dc23/eng/20250528

LC record available at https://lccn.loc.gov/2025013891

To

the next generation of

Black banjoists,

fiddlers,

guitarists,

bassists,

vocalists,

and musicians

carrying on the tradition

CONTENTS

ILLUSTRATIONS

MUSICAL TRANSCRIPTIONS AND BANJO TABLATURES

MUSICAL TRANSCRIPTIONS

BANJO TABLATURES

GO

BACK

AND

FETCH

IT

Understanding This Music

Afrofuturism asks us to imagine a future grounded in Black culture. But what about the past? As writer-musicians whose work is deeply grounded in history, we want to consider a past that is deeply centered in Black culture. How can we understand our collective history (and present, and future) differently if we start to imagine, as fully as possible, the rich tapestry of American culture that Black Americans wove? We might imagine a past where the dynamic sound of different African cultures meeting each other and European cultures in the Americas was made part of the historical record. Where people with power cared about African-derived musical forms and wrote down songs, asked people what lyrics meant, and saved instruments born of the African diaspora. Where people of African descent could write down records of their own music, rather than just having it filtered through the ears of people of European descent. This book will ask you to open your ears to that possibility, to imagine something broader than the scant historical record we have of Black American music before Emancipation in the United States, and to make this music live again in new, interesting ways.

In 1867, three abolitionists asked something similar in the wake of the Civil War. Lucy McKim Garrison, William Francis Allen, and Charles P. Ware compiled *Slave Songs of the United States*, the first collection of Black music in the United States. In their introduction, they questioned "why no systematic effort has hitherto been made to collect and preserve" the music of Black Americans. Slavery, racism, prejudice, and the withholding of education from Black people were the answers before 1865.[1] They were then entering a postslavery era with hopes of equality for Black Americans, and the editors of the collection hoped to make that systematic effort to preserve and disseminate the music of the formerly enslaved. However, they could only transcribe music they heard, or songs they received from friends and correspondents. A compiled historical record of Black music from before *Slave Songs* was missing then and has been missing—until now. In this book, we want to carry on the tradition of Allen, Ware, and McKim Garrison, and bring the sources of pre–Civil War Black music together as fully as possible.

However, our systematic effort still faces limitations. For one, almost all of the songs in the book you now hold—except the ones in *Slave Songs* and a few others—people saved almost by chance. They are brief illustrations in larger books that might not be about music at all; a scrawled notation in a manuscript that has been tucked away in an archive; a singular example of Black music standing alone in a published collection of material from the white canon; or a curiosity in a personal, hand-transcribed music manuscript. They were never collected to prove a point or preserve Black music, as *Slave Songs* did.

We know that people of African descent so visibly and frequently made music that musicality became one of the stereotypes of Blackness. Yet the lack of historical material is another major limitation we have in trying to uncover what music people of African descent played in the Americas. And the paucity is striking. In European countries such as Sweden or Ireland, you might find tens of thousands of folk tunes that date to before the mid-nineteenth century. But besides *Slave Songs*, we only know of fewer than ten songs definitively from the African American tradition transcribed in the United States before 1861. We can imagine that each community of enslaved and free Black people had their own musical culture—songs and variations of songs—just as each community in Sweden has its own songs and variations of songs. What we are attempting becomes like musical archaeology—using a piece of an object, a fragment of material culture to reconstruct a whole civilization.

For us, that civilization is the landscape of Black music in the Americas, but another major limitation is simply defining what early Black music of the Americas is. Simply put, it is vernacular songs and tunes that people of African descent played in the Americas between 1687 and 1865.

We opened our vision past the borders of the present-day United States not only because of the very few examples we listed above but because we want to acknowledge that the United States has never been physically or culturally separate from the Caribbean. In the civilization we are re-creating, we know that people of African descent came together to create new African American cultures, which you could see in new modes of dress, taste in new foodways, speak in new languages, and hear in new music. People were taken from Africa, and then they and their descendants were transported willingly and unwillingly across national borders, from colonies to countries, bringing with them new music and new musical instruments that had been created in the Americas. In the 1770s, English doctor William Dickson transcribed a work chant in Barbados (Piece 2), not unlike the work song from Virginia "Round the Corn, Sally!" (Piece 12b), which appears in *Slave Songs*. On Saint-Barthélemy in the Caribbean, Swedish doctor Christopher Carlander transcribed a song called "Black Dance" (Piece 6) in 1788, a version of which Albany, New York, resident Elizabeth Sanders Van Rensselaer transcribed in her music book around the same time. In 1814, a white planter heard "Aia bombaia bombé" (Piece 8) in Haiti, a chant similar to one heard in Albany ten years earlier. These musical examples show the connection between these places and how African musical traditions remained while distinct American traditions emerged.

However, in all but three instances, the songs in this book were written down by white people for white audiences, and the remaining three made by Black men were transcribed for white American or European audiences. We therefore have to consider the transmission of musical traditions between people of African descent and people of European descent, and the process of creolization in music.[2] First, we have to acknowledge that people in Africa heard European music and people in Europe heard African music before the beginning of the Atlantic slave trade.[3] In the Americas, free and enslaved Black musicians, especially fiddlers, played for white people, from the Caribbean to New York, in formal and informal settings, as soon as people were forcibly taken from Africa to the Americas.

By the 1770s, European and European-descended observers in the Americas tried to distinguish between what they saw as African traditions of the enslaved and free people of color and those that had been influenced by European culture. They weren't particularly rigorous in their assessments, however. For example, President Thomas Jefferson thought that the banjo was "brought hither from Africa," and in *History, Civil and Commercial, of the British Colonies in the West Indies*, Bryan Edwards, who was born in England but owned people and estates in Jamaica, commented that the instruments of the enslaved in Jamaica included "the Banja or Merriwang, the Dundo, and the Goombay; all of African origin."[4] They didn't have enough experience with Africa or African cultures to realize two important facts: that the banjo was not an African instrument but an African American invention constructed unlike any African instrument; and that the songs and dances they heard and saw were not direct transplants from any one African culture but the product of creolized African and European cultures.

Appearing in published and unpublished collections of music starting in the 1780s, tunes such as "Pompey Ran Away" (Piece 5), "Black Dance" (Piece 6), and "Congo" (Piece 7) show that white musicians were either playing tunes from the African American tradition, or trying to emulate music from African American musicians. The rise of Blackface performance beginning in the mid-1820s through the explosion of Blackface Minstrelsy in the early-1840s put Black music in the ears of white Americans and made banjos a widespread instrument.[5] However, the self-created mythology of the Minstrels has always made it hard to parse what songs were actually from the African American tradition and which ones were invented for the sake of show business. "Throw the Banjo Out of Tune" (Piece 11a) and "Snowden's Jig" (Piece 13) show us that at least some Minstrels did hear and transcribe Black music.

Another problem of musical transcription is a problem of musical literacy. Whatever you might call this music—folk, traditional, or vernacular—it isn't necessarily supposed to be learned from written music because that writing limits what you can actually capture about the tune or song. So many people who can sing or play instruments cannot read so-called standard Western European music notation and don't need to. Those who can read music may be able to transcribe or write music, but for many musicians, this takes time, close listening, and their preferred instrument close at hand to sound out the notes. It is truly a gift or hard-earned skill to be able to hear a melody a few times and then write out the notes on treble clef. When Lucy McKim went to South Carolina in 1862, she was working as a piano teacher and had extensive classical training. She was able to write down the melodies of "Poor Rosy" (Piece 12a) and other songs as she heard them. Others in the Sea Islands simply wrote down lyrics because they did not have that skill. Similarly, the Black man named Mr. Baptiste who transcribed "Angola" (Piece 1a), "Papa" (Piece 1b), and "Koromanti" (Piece 1c) in Jamaica was a professional musician, likely trained in the Catholic Church. Solomon Northrup learned to play and sing "Roaring River" (Piece 9) after he was captured as a free professional musician and sold into slavery in Louisiana, and he wrote the song out after he was freed from his enslavement. As Black men, Northup, Mr. Baptiste, and H. C. Focke ("Tárawan sa de," Piece 10) are the outliers of people who made transcriptions of Black music.

The oppression of people of African descent in the Americas kept them from making contemporary records of their own music, but Black people have kept musical records through oral and auditory transmission over generations. This type of transmission is common in what we often call folk music across the world, and a lot of folk music—even if it is from Europe—does not fit nicely in standard notation. Some might argue that it shouldn't even be attempted to be transcribed in that way because the rhythms, lilts, and stresses simply do not fit on something designed for Western European liturgical music. However, the standard notation allows us to analyze music and play it hundreds of years after it was written. We also know that a strictly auditory transmission over time presents a problem for researchers. Music, like any cultural product, changes over generations, and even from musician to musician based on their interests and proclivities, which gives us new tunes but does not necessarily preserve the old.

As we approach this music from both scholarly and music-making perspectives, we have to consider what creolized African American music might have sounded like through a triangulation of contemporaneous—often white but sometimes Black—observers and what we know about African musical traditions. For one, African music is participatory: anyone and everyone can be a part of it.[6] In the headnote to Baptiste's transcriptions of Black music in Jamaica, from 1687 (chapter 1), Hans Sloane writes that "you must clap Hands when the Base is plaid, and cry, *Alla, Alla*," suggesting that everyone is a part of the chorus. Although descriptions of specific dances vary, people could join in a dance if they felt compelled.[7] In Barbados, Dr. George Pinckard wrote that two (or sometimes up to four) people dance at a time, "until one is tired, and when this [*sic*] escapes from the circle another assumes the place, thus continuing to follow, one by one, in succession, so as frequently to keep up the dance, without any interval, for several hours."[8] There is no real audience; everyone can be part of the music, even if they are just clapping their hands or singing a chorus, and anyone can join in to dance.[9]

African music is also in essence dance music, and many examples of Black music in the Americas are related to dancing, both secular and religious.[10] The secular dances include contra dances and dances with set figures and steps, which would have been danced to the Jamaican "Calemba" (Piece 4a) and Barthélemois "Black Dance" (Piece 6). Secular dances had a long and continuous history of being danced by people of African descent in the Americas. In the 1690s, Father Jean-Baptiste Labat reported that the priests taught enslaved people in Martinique "several French dances such as the minuet, la courante, la passe-pied, and others, as well as 'les branles' [a type of circle or line dance] and round dances" so that they would stop dancing the religious Calinda. Nearly 150 years later, Cynric Williams toured Jamaica in the years before the British abolition of slavery and saw Black men and women dancing "country-dances and quadrilles" to the music of "three fiddles, a pipe and tabor, and a triangle." Jigs, including "Pompey Ran Away" (Piece 5), "Congo" (Piece 7), and "Snowden's Jig" (Piece 13), are also secular dance tunes. In the Americas, jigs were a mix of step dancing from the British Isles (which might have been influenced by French court dances) and African-derived dance steps. Dance historian Phil Jamison writes that while jigs were typically in 6/8 time, jigs did not have to be in 6/8 time but could just mean a "fast and lively dance."[11]

Many of the songs in this collection are also religious, even if they were played during a dance. Music and dance are also so integral to West African religions that some scholars refer to them as "danced religions." Dances could connect people to ancestors, gods, and spirits.[12] "Angola" (Piece 1a), "Papa" (Piece 1b), "The Colymba" (Piece 4b), "Aia bombaia

Merrymaking at a Wayside Inn, attributed to John Lewis Krimmel, ca. 1811–1813. Although the fiddler is somewhat caricatured, Krimmel was one of the first artists in the United States to paint multiple scenes of the lives of free Black Americans. Here, a Black fiddler plays for white dancers at an inn. Rogers Fund, 1942, Metropolitan Museum of Art, New York.

bombé" (Piece 8), and "Tárawan sa de" (Piece 10) are part of the religious dance tradition often danced on Sundays and holidays. These dances allowed people to gather and worship ancestors, grieve lost loved ones, and pray for better conditions. Sometimes they also allowed enslaved people to plot subversive or rebellious activity outside the gaze of white enslavers. And yet, as dangerous as the dances could be, enslavers would still allow them to happen. As the famed abolitionist Frederick Douglass, who escaped from slavery, wrote, "These holidays serve as conductors, or safety-valves, to carry off the rebellious spirit of enslaved humanity," and he believed these holidays "to be among the most effective means in the hands of the slaveholder in keeping down the spirit of insurrection."[13] They could also be an opportunity to begin an insurrection—as with the music performed before the Stono Rebellion in South Carolina in 1739.

We have also included work songs in this collection, including "An African Song or Chant" from Barbados (Piece 2), "Poor Rosy" (Piece 12a), and "Round the Corn, Sally!" (12b). These are characterized by their call-and-response singing and were used to determine the cadence of work, whether it was the rowing of oars or grinding of corn. Observed among enslaved people of African descent in the Americas as early as 1640, call-and-response song is recognized as a hallmark of African American song and can be heard in Central African *ngolo* fight-dancing and West African dance, religious, and social music.[14] This call-and-response form could also be used in invocation in African-diasporic religious ceremonies including Cuban Santería, Haitian Vodou, Brazilian Candomblé, and Surinamese Winti.[15]

Despite the many limitations of uncovering early Black music, we hope musicians today will learn these tunes and embody their history. In the historical headnotes to the music, we provide more substance about how the songs were collected and by whom. We also want these songs to be accessible to musicians in the twenty-first century, so that we can hear them come alive in living rooms, at music camps, on front porches, and in ballrooms across the country and world. For this reason, we're including both standard notation and banjo tablature.

Although only some of the songs in this book were noted as being performed by banjoists, we've chosen to include banjo tab for the pieces to acknowledge the importance of the banjo in Black musical traditions of the Americas and to make the music accessible to banjo players who cannot read standard notation. The banjo tabs were written for downstroke playing (sometimes called clawhammer or stroke style). As you, players and readers, learn this music and these techniques, perhaps you will find a way that these pieces fit into your downstroke, two-finger, or three-finger banjo playing.

The banjo was created in the Americas by people of African descent and became hugely important to Black religious and spiritual practice before becoming an instrument of social dance.[16] This banjo was also very different from our contemporary banjos. Until the nineteenth century, the banjo was made of a gourd or calabash body where the side had been cut off and covered in animal skin, and it is most often described as having four strings. The instrument also wasn't one of a string ensemble. In all but one account of the banjo before the 1770s, the instrument is played solo or, more often, with drums. The dances that the banjo accompanies are also not the secular set-style or jig dances (which had a fiddle accompaniment) but rather religious dances that white observers thought of as more "African" than "European."

The standard notation transcriptions make the music legible and playable for any musician or vocalist who can read it and are as exact to the original transcriptions as possible. We are especially considering the Black fiddle tradition with this notation. Black musicians played the violin for dances that had a social function.[17] When traveling in the West Indies in the 1790s, Dr. George Pinckard distinguished that at the "cabins," enslaved people danced to "the song of the rude African drum, the rattle, and the banjar," while in "the great hall of the government house," they danced to "a violin, with the fife and drum for their band."[18] Black fiddlers would play for both white and Black dances, as exemplified by Christopher Carlander's account in Saint-Barthélemy and "Black Dance" (Piece 6) and Solomon Northrup's "Roaring River" (Piece 9). Early historical accounts also indicate that fiddles and banjos were not played together—that phenomenon is something we first see appear en masse with Blackface Minstrelsy even among African Americans.[19]

In the historical record, percussion was actually the most common instrument played by people of African descent in the Americas, present in accounts of both religious dances (together with the banjo) and secular dances (with the fiddle). Rhythm could come from body percussion (patting juba or clapping); handheld rattles or rattles tied to the body; tambourines or handheld drums; a board hit with sticks called a *quaqua*; a triangle; a jar or gourd hit on the opening with a hand; a square frame covered in skin called a goombay drum; a large drum open on one end that a player would sit on; or a drum held between the legs.

African rhythms were not easy for European transcribers to understand, and only one of these musical examples had specific notations of the rhythm, made by H. C. Focke, who was of European and African descent. Western European music places the stress on the downbeat (in 4/4 time, this is ONE-two-three-four), while African music doesn't necessarily follow that pattern.[20] The "standard pattern" of African rhythm—two quarter notes, one eighth note, three quarter notes, one eighth note—is written out over 12/8 time, meaning that the eighth note gets the beat and there are twelve eighth notes in a measure.[21] This doesn't fit evenly on 2/4 or 4/4 time, which can make it hard for people unfamiliar with the pattern to feel the rhythm. But when the "standard pattern" is played against melodies written in 2/4 or 4/4 time (as many of the pieces in this collection are), you get a natural syncopation. This syncopation is a feeling of anticipation that creates forward propulsion as a melody is repeated over and over again.[22]

Audiences unfamiliar with three-against-two time and syncopation not only can't find the beat and don't understand this dynamism but can experience the rhythm as monotonous (without enough going on) or cacophonous (with too much going on). Many European observers of Black music in the Americas related those feelings. In Martinique in the late 1600s, priest Jean-Baptiste Labat experienced alienation; during the Calinda dance, he wrote, the player of a larger drum keeps an even rhythm, while the baboula player "beats as fast as he can," which "only serves to make noise."[23] Labat can't hear the rhythm, but there probably was one.[24] In Suriname, John Gabriel Stedman noted that people of African descent "always use full, or half measure, but never triple time, in their dancing music" and that the drum "sounds tuckety-tuck tuckety-tuck, ad perpetuum," offering a rhythmic idea without much detail.[25] Understanding how important rhythm was to this music, we should explore their accompaniment with any number of percussive instruments, from feet via percussive dance to tambourines to drums.

In this book, we want to highlight Black song, fiddle playing, and percussion in addition to Black banjo playing. We hope that by containing as much of this music as we can in one place, patterns of tunings, rhythms, melodies, and lyrics will emerge and that these may be able to shed light on what we know and still have to learn about early Black music in the Americas and how it was foundational to American music. We want the sounds that were once heard across the Americas, from Suriname in South America through the Caribbean to the southern United States and as far north as New York, to become part of the musical canon of American music once again.

Enslaved People Making Music, Théodore Bray, 1850. A drawing of some of the percussion instruments used in Black music before the 1860s in Suriname. Wereldmuseum Amsterdam, Netherlands.

Playing This Music

BY RHIANNON GIDDENS

In general, musical transcriptions are an act of creativity, deeply rooted in the knowledge of the person doing the transcribing. You can never discount how decades of experience can shape how we think of the music when we are writing it down. How a person has been trained—whether with paper or by ear, in a class or by apprenticeship—heavily impacts everything from where they feel the pulse to how they think of the rhythm and where they place the downbeat. In banjo tab notation, slurs, hammer ons, and pull offs can shift the feel of a piece depending on where they are placed, without ever changing a note.

Basically, one needs to own their perspective. Although the standard notations in this book are naturally influenced by my experience, you are free to compare them to the handwritten or typed originals of the music. They are intended to be a faithful transcription of the originals rather than an artistic interpretation. This original notation does not exist for the banjo, though. To aid modern banjo players in resurrecting this music, we've chosen to include banjo tabs. These tabs truly are an act of creativity, based on my decades of experience with African American banjo playing and historic tunes written for the banjo. But the creativity shows itself more in the choice of articulation, rather than the notes, which are meant to represent as best as I can what is in the original transcription, albeit often in a key more appropriate for my banjo.

I am a classically trained opera singer who picked up the modern banjo in my twenties. The banjo is an instrument I learned by ear and from different people over the space of years before eventually apprenticing with the African American old-time fiddler Joe Thompson. He was eighty-six and the last of his family to play a type of banjo-led North Carolina string band music that was already old when he was learning it as a boy. The foundation of how I approach the banjo, and how I play old-time music, was heavily shaped by playing with Joe and with the two young musicians also there to learn from him, and it has colored all the folk music I have learned and played since.

The five-string banjo has a short drone string that creates a kind of syncopation just by dint of existing, and in the years that I developed my playing by accompanying Joe, I found myself accenting it naturally stronger than in the usual style of clawhammer banjo found in old-time music. That preference for the short string comes through in the banjo tab transcriptions in this book.

Some years ago, I discovered the early banjo, commonly called the Minstrel banjo, and started to learn that playing technique. I bought banjo tutors from the 1850s and 1860s that had been put into tab by modern scholars. I began to learn the specific licks and techniques unique to that era of banjo playing, which had largely died out in five-string banjo playing as it shifted to noncommercial, rural types of playing. More so than contemporary old-time or clawhammer banjo playing, this mid-nineteenth-century downstroke style, I've found, allows me to better play many of the tunes in this book.

This means that the tunings for the banjo, unless otherwise noted, are the relative pitches of what is called Classic C. Most banjoists today will be familiar with G tuning (gDGBD), and Classic C lowers the fourth string (lowest string) a whole step so that the strings are tuned gCGBD. In the mid-nineteenth century, banjos were pitched lower, and so on a gourd or mid-nineteenth-century-style wooden-rim banjo these relative pitches would be cFCEG or eAEG♯B. Some of the banjo pieces are in the tuning that Frank Converse described a Black banjo player using ("Throw the Banjo Out of Tune," Piece 11a), with the second string raised a half step to eAEAB (which I play in cFCFG). The most important thing is that the pitch relationship between the strings follows Classic C or Classic C with the second string raised a whole step.[1] For banjoists to play with the transcriptions, we've either marked my tuning or the alternate modern tuning with an asterisk (*) or added the appropriate tuning.

A final note on the sound. The early banjo looks the same as the modern banjo in basic shape and technology, but it has quite a different feel and sound. The skin is real, not synthetic; the hoop is made of wood with relatively little metal, and the strings are animal gut rather than metal. The instrument is larger, and most importantly, fretless and tuned a full fourth or fifth lower than the contemporary banjo. The strings are higher off the fretboard, and the give of gut or imitation gut strings is rather more extreme than the modern steel string. Before this era banjos would have been made from gourds instead of wooden hoops, but the feel of music on the instrument wouldn't have been extremely different. I encourage any banjo player who wants to play this era's music to consider getting or making a gourd banjo, or a Minstrel replica, as it will materially improve your chance of getting the feel available in these tunes.

I am using my experience on my Minstrel-era banjo (a replica made by Jim Hartel based on a banjo made by Levi Brown around 1858) and my gourd banjo to infer the best way to put some of these tunes into banjo tabs. I am also using a style of tab used by Joseph Weidlich, which combines modern banjo tab with Minstrel banjo–era notation. In this notation, each of the five strings is represented by a line on the staff, starting with the fifth (short) string as the lowest line. The number indicates the left-hand fret position (for example, 1 equals first fret). Below the staff, the × signifies that the note is played with the thumb and the • signifies that the note is played with the index finger. The ⌒ indicates a hammer or a pull off with the left hand, and if it includes an arrow, it indicates that a left-hand finger glides between adjacent strings (for example, striking the second string and then gliding to strike the first string). Except for "Throw the Banjo Out of

Tune" (Piece 11a) and "So Come Along" (Piece 11b), we don't know whether the music was intended to be played on banjo. Therefore, the source itself doesn't indicate any fingerings and what is written in the banjo tab are my choices. The use of the thumb versus the index finger is an ergonomic and stylistic choice, and some players might find variations that work better for them.

Last, we want you to think of how and why you are playing these pieces today. They can serve as a window into the past, but they can also be a blueprint for future music. The songs don't have to be played by banjo and fiddle or a string band of banjo-fiddle-guitar-bass. Some come alive with percussion, a flat-picked guitar, or vocals. For example, when I play some of these with West African or Mediterranean percussion, different aspects of the rhythm are highlighted, leading me to new ways of thinking about how I play these tunes on the banjo. How you wish to adapt and transform the originals, transcriptions, or banjo tabs is your act of creativity.

CHAPTER

Angola, Papa, and Koromanti

JAMAICA, 1687–1688

By the accounting of British doctor Hans Sloane, Mr. Baptiste was the best musician Sloane encountered at a festival in Jamaica during his visit to the Caribbean island in 1687–88.[1] So Sloane asked Baptiste to transcribe some of the music being played by Black musicians there.

Baptiste transcribed "Angola," "Papa," and "Koromanti," which appear in a two-page spread in Sloane's book *A Voyage to the Islands Madera, Barbados, Nieves, S. Christophers and Jamaica* (1707). Baptiste was of African descent, and he knew how to read and write music, something he may have learned training as a musician in the Catholic Church. He could take what some white people described as a bestial howl or music without much variety and turn it into melodies and harmonies and vocal lines and instrumental accompaniment.[2] Baptiste's notations are the earliest known transcription of Black music in the Americas.

Sloane offered no more about Baptiste's background than his ability as a musician, and it is only through archival research that scholars have been able to learn more about who he was. Still, no one has yet been able to find a transcription of the music in Baptiste's handwriting or any additional notes from Sloane about Baptiste or the music. Researchers dream of a moment of finding something like this, which would illuminate more about these songs or perhaps even show the differences between the original handwritten transcription and the published version. For now, we assume that what Sloane published in his book was an accurate transcription of Baptiste's words and notes.

The titles of the pieces "Angola," "Papa," and "Koromanti" share names with African communities or ethnic groups, in which case they may be named for the people who performed the music, but the names of African music can also reference an instrument or dance.[3] "Angola" may refer to Bantu-speaking people from the kingdom of Ngola, which the Portuguese colonized in the late sixteenth century.[4] "Papa" may be a variant of Popo, another name for the Mina, who live along the coast of the Bight of Benin in eastern West Africa. "Koromanti" may refer to enslaved people who had origins in Akan communities to the west of the Bight of Benin along what Europeans called the Gold Coast.[5] In accounts from the same time (and later) that describe enslaved people gathering to play music and dance in spiritual festivals from Jamaica to New Orleans, white observers noted various "nations" or ethnic groups, and while they may have each had their own style of music and dance, they were not separate. In Sloane's account, we see different instruments, styles of music, and Black people of various cultural backgrounds coming together. This exemplifies the musical exchanges already underway in the Americas by the 1680s and how these traditions were not passed in their entirety from African cultures and were transforming into new African American cultures.[6]

Sloane also does not say which instruments would have played these melodies. He did, however, include an illustration in his book with three instruments: two banjos (which he calls "strum-strumps") and a harp. In his travels around the Americas in 1783–84, Johann David Schöpf noted that the banjo he observed was tuned "like a chord," which would require at least three strings.[7] With only three notes, the song "Papa" could easily be played on the banjos that Sloane collected in Jamaica, which are depicted with two strings. The eight-string harp in Sloane's illustration appears to be almost identical to the *sanko* harp of the central West African Asante people. Seeing *sanko* players in 1819, Thomas Edward Bowdich wrote that "airs on this instrument are played very quick, and it is barely possible to make even an experienced player lessen the time."[8] This harp may have been used for "Koromanti." The range of notes in "Koromanti" is harder to achieve on a two- or three-string banjo like the ones in Sloane's image. Furthermore, the rapid succession of notes would also have been more difficult on early gourd and calabash banjos, where the strings were higher off the fingerboard than contemporary banjos.

Sloane writes that enslaved people formerly played drums, but because drums

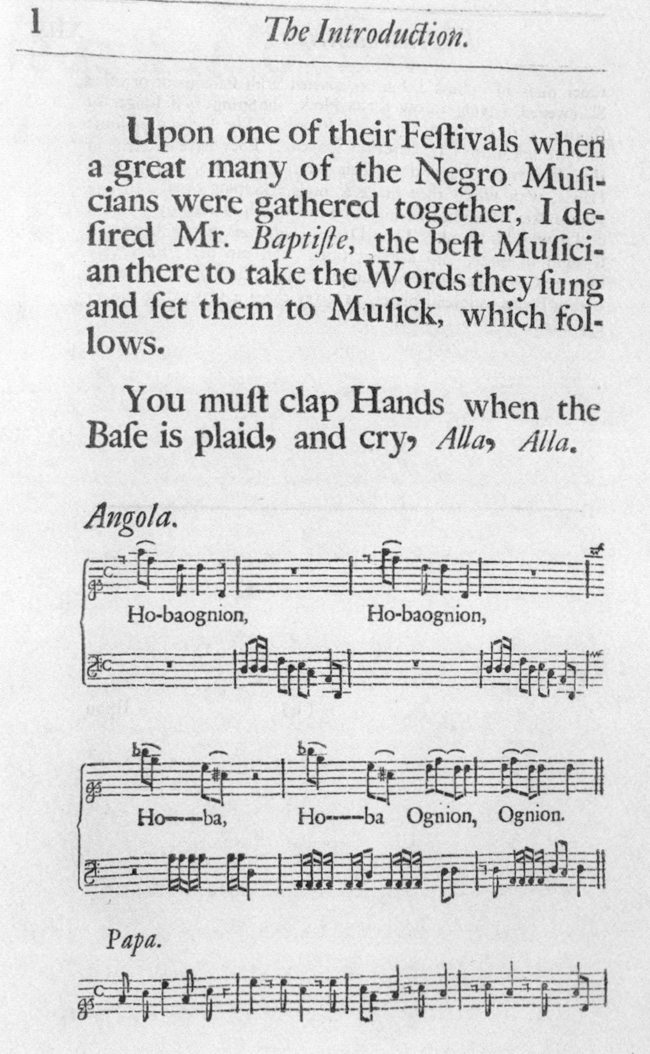
1 The Introduction.

Upon one of their Feſtivals when a great many of the Negro Muſicians were gathered together, I deſired Mr. *Baptiſte*, the beſt Muſician there to take the Words they ſung and ſet them to Muſick, which follows.

You muſt clap Hands when the Baſe is plaid, and cry, *Alla*, *Alla*.

The first page of transcriptions of Jamaican festival music in Hans Sloane's *Voyage to the Islands*, published in 1707 and based on his trip to the island in 1687–1688. James Ford Bell Library, University of Minnesota Libraries, Minneapolis.

might have incited rebellion, they were banned.[9] Instead, people have "Rattles ty'd to their Legs and Wrists, and in their Hands," and someone keeps time "on the mouth of an empty Gourd or Jar with his Hand."[10] Neither Baptiste nor Sloane notes what rhythms these instruments might have made, and European readers of Sloane's book are instead instructed to simply "clap Hands when the Base is plaid."[11] This clapping on the "Base" would have provided a two- or four-beat pulse.[12] With all the percussion instruments Sloane mentions at the festival and the importance of polyrhythm in African music, the people gathered at the festival in Jamaica would have played more than body percussion. Baptiste may not have been able to transcribe those beats, or those beats may have been improvised.

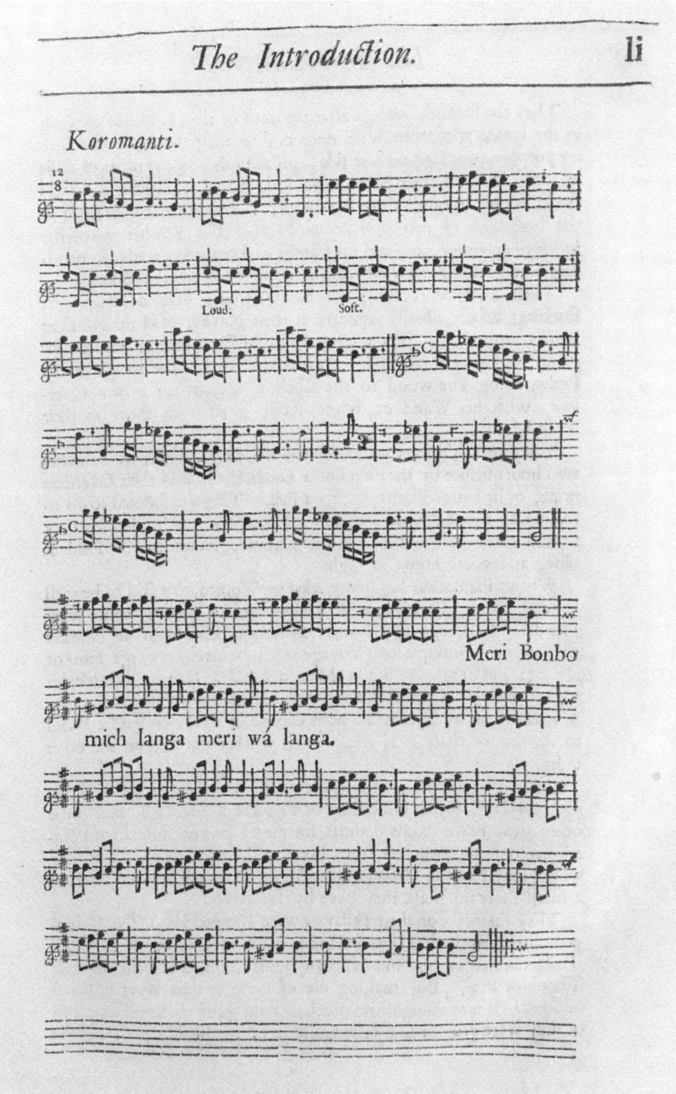

The second page of transcriptions from Hans Sloane's *Voyage to the Islands*. As a doctor, Sloane wrote mostly about natural history. No transcription in Mr. Baptiste's handwriting has been found. James Ford Bell Library, University of Minnesota Libraries, Minneapolis.

Sloane provided such scant information about the pieces that we do not know their purpose, but since they were played at a festival, they were likely part of a religious or spiritual ritual.

"Angola"

"Angola" is in 4/4 time and is the only piece with two parts, a vocal line in treble clef and what appears to be an instrumental line in bass clef. The phrase "Ho-baognion" is sung once, followed by what seems to be a response from an instrument over the course of a measure, then this call-and-response is repeated once more before the vocal line and instrument line play together. In Rhiannon's banjo tab, she has chosen to combine both lines into one banjo part. The original notation covers just over three and a half octaves, which would be challenging to play on the banjo, and Rhiannon has arranged it over one and a half octaves. Just as Mr. Baptiste made artistic choices when he took what he heard in Jamaica and transcribed it, so Rhiannon has made an artistic choice about how this piece could be played on solo banjo.

No one has been able to translate the lyrics to "Angola" from an African or American Creole language. We know from the many early words for *banjo*—including *banjeau*, *banjau*, *banjay*, *banjar*, *bania*, *bagna*, and *banger*—that

Europeans and European-descended Americans had difficulty in transliterating the creolized languages people of African descent spoke. Baptiste may have transliterated these words in a way that he thought English speakers might be able to read.

It is unclear why this is the first piece of the transcriptions, but many African-diasporic religious celebrations begin with an invocation to specific gods or spirits. Lyrics sung in Haitian Vodou are invocations calling to spirits and gods, and Legba is usually honored first. He is the guardian of the crossroads of the dead and the living and can allow other spirits and gods to enter the Vodou dance of the living.[13] In Suriname, the religious *Banyaprei* dances "start with one or more songs in honor of the earth mother," asking her permission to dance. Perhaps the lyrics in "Angola" are therefore an invocation, allowing the celebration in Jamaica to begin.[14]

"Papa"

"Papa" is a heavily syncopated four-measure tune without a vocal line. In exploring the music of the early Blackface Minstrels, musicologist Hans Nathan writes that eighth-rest followed by eighth-note rhythmic patterns in some tunes recorded by banjoist Daniel Decatur Emmett are "unusual and intriguing" compared to American and European music of the nineteenth century. Having these "hectic offbeat accentuations" against a stress on the downbeat essentially changes 2/4 time into 4/8 time.[15] Although "Papa" is notated in 4/4 time, the rhythm is much easier to conceptualize in 8/8 time. Even though all of the transcriptions in this book are in Western notation, we often see the transcribers struggling with rhythmic patterns that don't match idioms of Western music.

Notated in A minor, "Papa" uses the three notes of the chord—the root (in this case A), the minor third (C), and the fifth (E)—with a surprise fourth (D) at the end, which almost seems to signal a return to the beginning of the tune. In the banjo tab, on beats one and three in the first measure, Rhiannon indicates a • (index finger on the right hand striking the string) and an arrow, which indicates that she suggests gliding the first finger on the second string to the first finger on the first string. In measure four, Rhiannon transposes the last eighth note of the measure up an octave from the original notation. This adds to the feeling that the piece needs to be repeated before ending on the lower octave.

"Koromanti"

Although the second page of Baptiste's transcriptions is labeled "Koromanti," it seems to be made up of three distinct pieces. "Koromanti One" is in C major and 12/8 time; "Koromanti Two" is in D minor and 4/4 time; and "Koromanti Three" is in B minor and without a time signature.

The 12/8 time signature of "Koromanti One" means that each measure is made of twelve eighth notes, and they are notated in four groups of three. This makes it unique among the songs Baptiste notated for Sloane and unusual for any African American music notated before the 1860s. For instance, all of the songs collected for the collection *Slave Songs of the United States* are in 2/4 or 4/4 time, save for a few in 6/8 and 3/4. Furthermore, even though in "Koromanti One" the beats are broken down into sets of three notes, the emphasis is on the beat, a striking contrast with the offbeat stresses in "Papa." As notated, "Koromanti One" does not have the cross- or counterrhythms usually associated with African music. However, a percussionist could easily create that.[16] The "standard pattern" in African rhythms is based around a 12/8 time, so perhaps already here we see a creolization of African rhythms coming together with European-inspired melodies.[17]

"Koromanti Two" begins with a fast scale descending from a high G, which repeats four times throughout the piece. This may be an instrumental piece ideally suited for the harp Sloane collected.

Mr. Baptiste didn't write a time signature for "Koromanti Three," which might be because more so than the other pieces, measure and beat delineations don't seem to make sense for the piece. However, the banjo tab is notated in 4/4. The first four measures seem like a call-and-response, and these melodies reappear throughout the piece, slightly altered in rhythm or transposed to a lower register than the rest of the piece. Four measures in, Mr. Baptiste writes the lyrics, "Meri Bonbo mich langa meri wa langa." Like the lyrics "Ho-baognion" in "Angola," we have no translation.

If all we had were Mr. Baptiste's transcriptions from Jamaica in 1687, we could still learn a lot about the transformation of African musical traditions to African American music. For example, a creolization of language was already taking place within the musical sphere. The lyrics Mr. Baptiste transcribes ("Ho-baognion" and "Meri

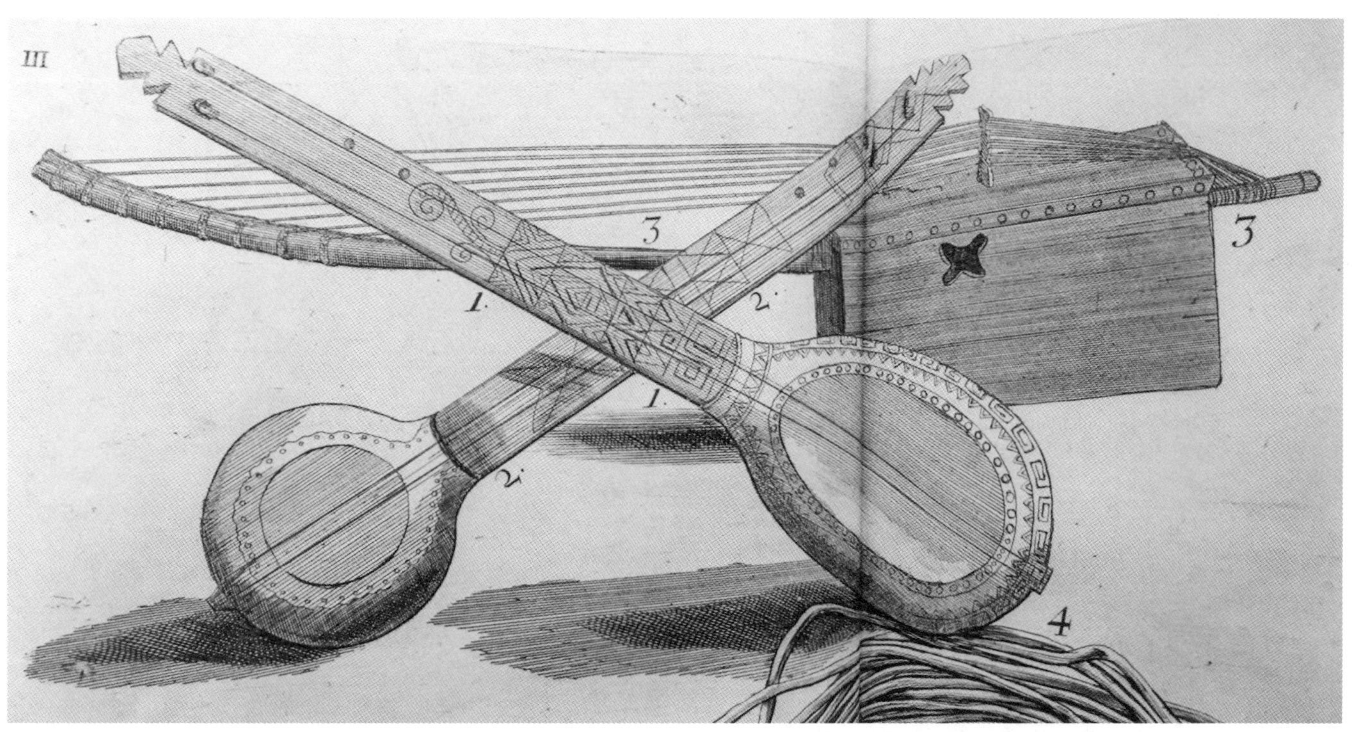

Hans Sloane collected two banjos and a harp in Jamaica and had the instruments engraved in his book *A Voyage to the Islands*. However, he did not say which instruments were played for which pieces. James Ford Bell Library, University of Minnesota Libraries, Minneapolis.

Bonbo mich langa meri wa langa") have not been identified as any African language or as Jamaican Patwah, suggesting that they may be a precursor to the creole spoken in Jamaica or another creole language altogether lost. We also don't know whether the lyrics from the two songs are in the same language. While the rhythmic patterns of the piece "Papa" feel polyrhythmic and non-European, scholars have pointed out that parts of "Koromanti" seem to resemble European lute music from the late seventeenth century.[18] Within the same festival, it appears we are witnessing multiple cultures coming together. ☙

ANGOLA

TRANSCRIPTION

cFCFG (As played by Rhiannon Giddens)
gCGCD (Alternate modern tuning)
aDADE (To play with transcription)

TABLATURE

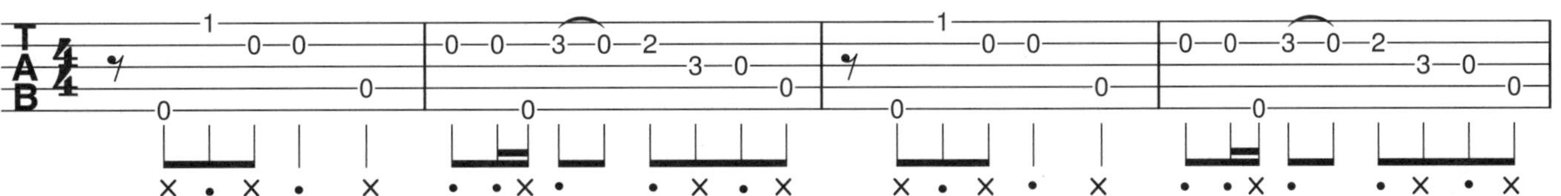

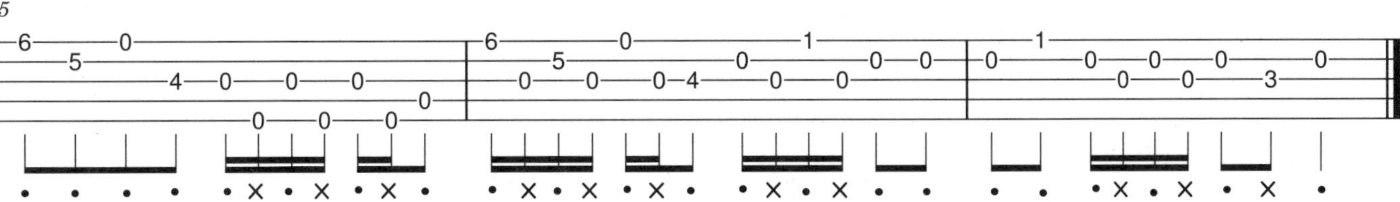

PAPA

TRANSCRIPTION

cFCEG (As played by Rhiannon Giddens)
gCGBD (Alternate modern tuning)
eAEG♯B (To play with transcription)

TABLATURE

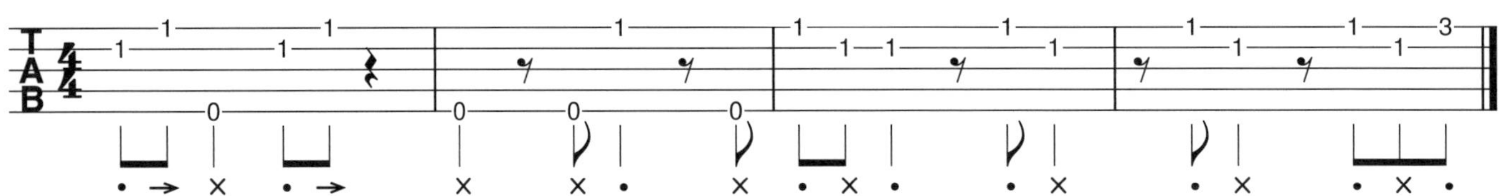

KOROMANTI

TRANSCRIPTION

KOROMANTI 1

cFCEG (As played by Rhiannon Giddens)
gCGBD (Alternate modern tuning)*

TABLATURE

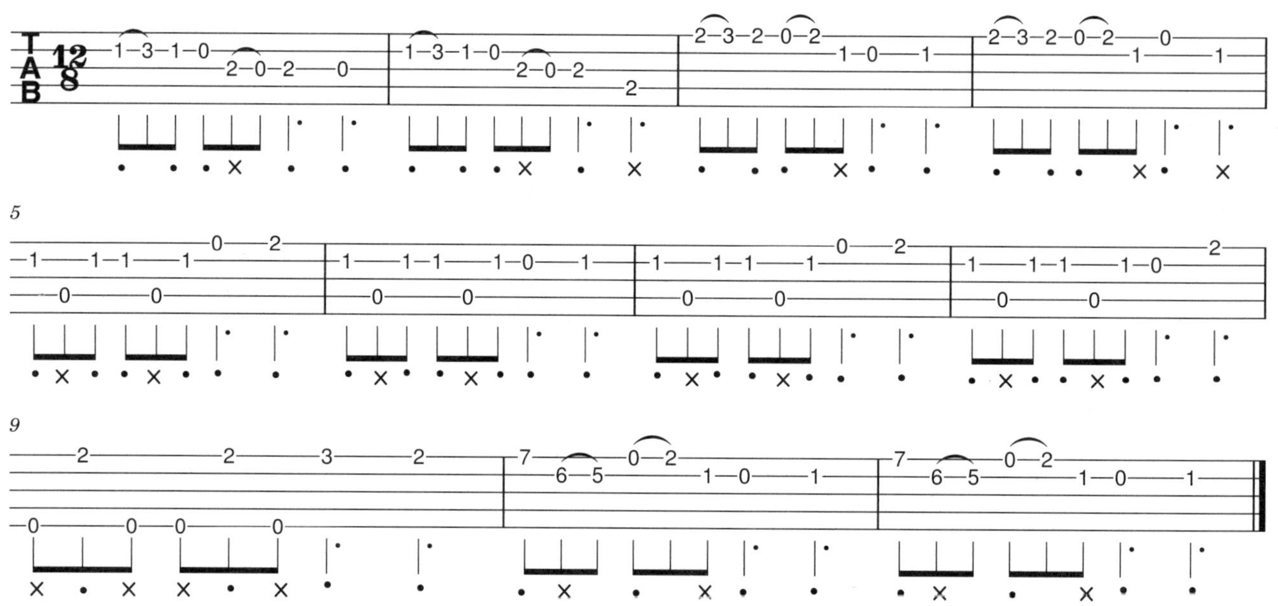

KOROMANTI 2

cFCFG (As played by Rhiannon Giddens)
gCGCD (Alternate modern tuning)*

TABLATURE

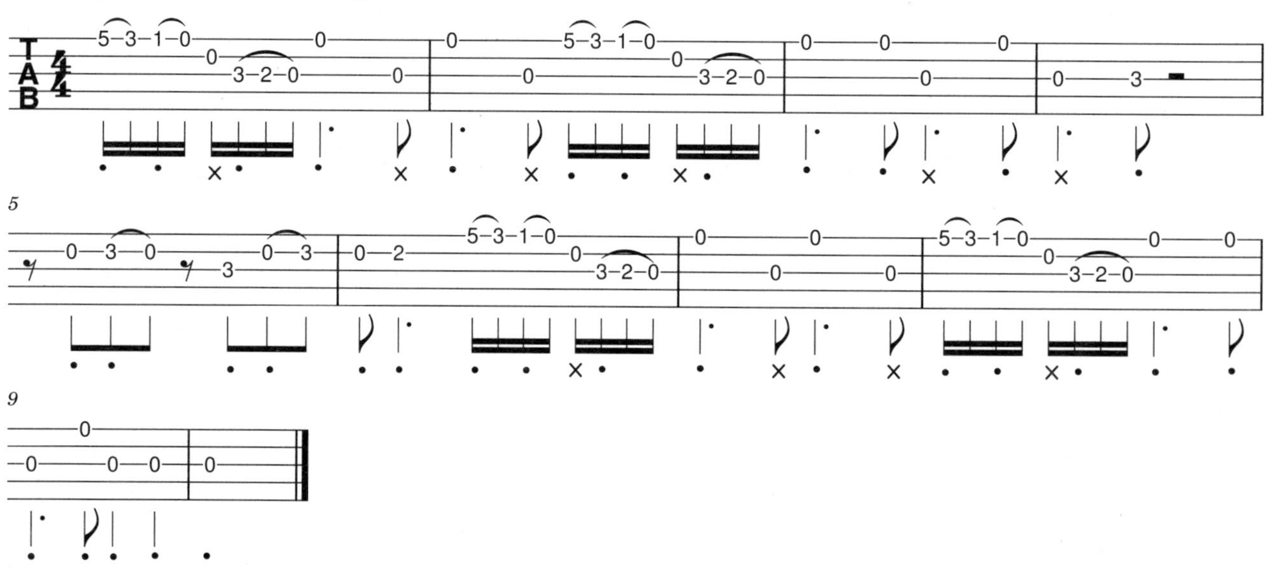

KOROMANTI 3

TABLATURE

cFCEG (As played by Rhiannon Giddens)
gCGBD (Alternate modern tuning)*

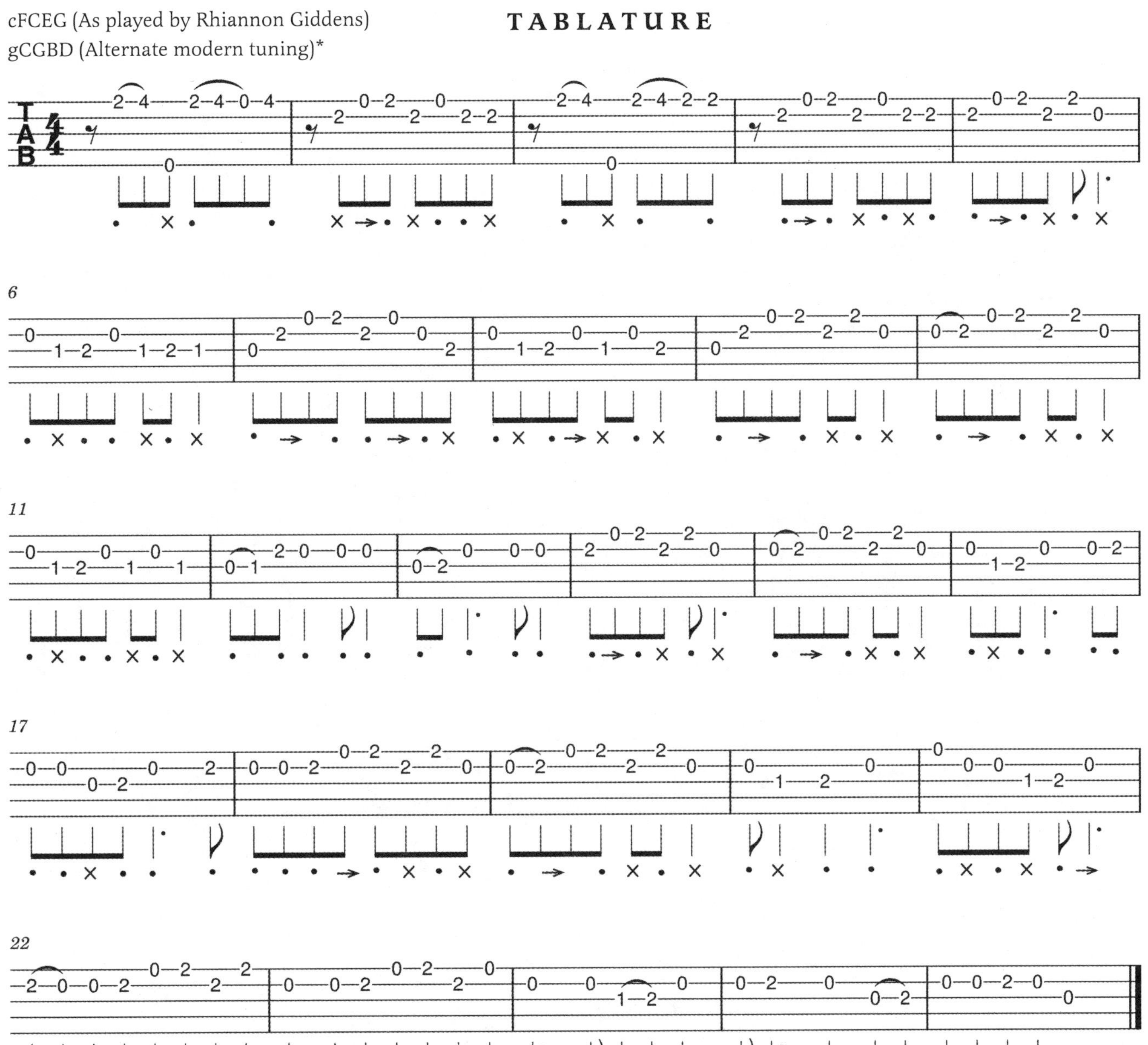

Enslaved people dancing and making music in Barbados from John Waller's *A Voyage in the West Indies*, 1820. Wellcome Collection, London, UK.

CHAPTER

An African Song or Chant

BARBADOS, CA. 1772–1779

By 1772, nearly a hundred years after Hans Sloane visited Jamaica, the scene he described of enslaved people dancing on Sundays was common in the Caribbean and North America. In Barbados, the white Scottish doctor William Dickson would approach the people dancing to get a better look. Men and women wore their best attire: jackets and dresses, hats and scarves, maybe beads hanging from their necks but twined around their arms and legs, too. The crowd could be huge, hundreds of people, and a ring of dancers would form, with people stepping into the center of the ring to dance solo before returning to the outside again. They'd often dance to drums, rattles, and banjos, though sometimes just drums and fiddles would suffice.[1] They might drink wine or rum and eat cakes given to them by an overseer or their owner.[2]

Dickson lived in Barbados for a number of years and served as the personal secretary of Governor Edward Hay.[3] Dickson became familiar enough with the enslaved people making music that they might invite him to join in the dancing, yet he wrote down only one song from his sojourn in the British colony, a work song that he called "An African Song or Chant."[4]

Dickson was impressed that the people of African descent he met in Barbados not only enjoyed music but had a "proficiency" that didn't come from formal instruction. They primarily played the *coromantin* drum (a drum that may have originated with the Koromanti of West Africa) and the *banjay*, the word he uses for banjo and later describes as "a rude kind of guitar." Although he calls the banjo "rude," he also says the instruments were as impressive as the "ancient [European] musical instruments."[5]

Whereas other observers might focus on music to prove that enslaved people were happy or simple, and thereby argue for the continuation of slavery, after years in Barbados, Dickson wished to use descriptions of the music of the enslaved to do the opposite. In 1789, he published *Letters on Slavery*, in which he hoped to prove the equality of people of African descent.[6] While the so-called Founding Fathers of the United States wrote that “all men are created equal” and yet still legalized slavery, Dickson and others in Britain were beginning a movement for abolition and Black equality.[7] In *Letters on Slavery*, Dickson asserted that enslaved people’s “taste for melody and harmony, if it does not demonstrate their rationality, ought, at least, to be admitted as an argument in providing their *humanity*.”[8]

The transcription of “An African Song or Chant” was made by Granville Sharp, considered a founder of the British abolition movement.[9] We don’t know whether Dickson made a quick transcription of the song while in Barbados and then passed that on to Sharp or if he remembered the melody and words and had Sharp write it down. There is, however, a first version, a second version, and a final version, suggesting that Dickson worked with Sharp on refining the transcription.[10] Dickson may have remembered this song more easily than other music he heard because work songs were meant to be learned on the spot.

Although there is no notated time signature, the notes are divided into 4/4 time. Like John Gabriel Stedman’s transcription of “A Black Soldier’s Song” (Piece 3), it seems as though the singer could hold on to notes, especially at the end of a phrase, if he or she chose to do so. Accounts from Barbados suggest that both men and women could serve as the leader of a song.[11]

The transcription for “An African Song or Chant,” with the note that it was “taken down in notes by G. S. [Granville Sharp] from the information of Dr. Wm. Dickson.” D3549/13/3/27, Gloucestershire Archives, UK.

Some researchers have also suggested that this work song is unique to the culture that existed during Bahamian slavery, because contemporary "Barbadian folk songs . . . privilege the major key," whereas this is in a minor key.[12]

Dickson or Sharp wrote that a single person "(while at Work with the rest of the Gang) leads the Song, and the others join in Chorus at the end of each verse," in a call-and-response format.[13] The lead singer begins, "Massa buy me he won't killa me," possibly a hopeful statement that an enslaver wouldn't destroy their own property. The singer repeats that line twice more, then sings, "'for he kill me he ship me regulaw," maybe suggesting that he would be sold before he was killed. The second verse reiterates that the enslaver is not a good white man:

'For I live with a bad Man, oh la,
'for I live with a *bad* man *Obudda bo*,
'For I live with a bad Man, oh la,
'for I would go to the Riverside Regulaw.

The last verse may imply that before you live with a bad master, you would go to your death and the world of the ancestors willingly. Water and waterways were deeply tied to Black religion and spiritual practice across the Americas, with water dividing the space of the living and the dead as a place where deities such as Wata Mama in the Surinamese Winti religion can live.[14] Dickson and Sharp also provide a chorus that enslaved people might sing "as they proceed in their work": an "ah" sound that follows a melody. Although it is a song that might control the cadence of work, the lyrics are also subversive, reflecting how many enslaved people died of overwork and how cruel enslavers were.

AN AFRICAN SONG OR CHANT

CHAPTER

A Black Soldier's Song

SURINAME, 1770S

"ONE BUSS, good-bye, o 'tis so," a Black soldier sings to his love in the colony of Suriname. He's dressed in a red cap—to be easily distinguished from the Black rebels—and blue pants. He has a weapon, too; although he's enslaved, he is trusted enough to have a gun. The soldier has been forced to fight against the Maroons, self-liberated people of African descent who created communities in the jungle of Suriname. The Maroons had been raiding and attacking plantations to free more enslaved people, creating a threat for the enslavers and government of the colony, which was owned by the city of Amsterdam and the Dutch West India Company. So, the government enlisted enslaved men such as the singer and white mercenaries from Europe to fight the Maroons.

One of the mercenaries was a Scottish Dutch soldier named John Gabriel Stedman, who wrote down those lyrics as part of "A Black Soldier's Song." In the memoir he later wrote, he explained that "as a specimen of [their vocal melodies] I will try to put the following notes to music, supposing a soldier going off to battle is taking leave of his mistress," and then transcribed a short two-line song on treble clef notation.[1]

Stedman had received an education in art and music and played the fiddle and the flute, and the music in Suriname was of constant interest to him. He was able to offer information on Surinamese musical culture not just because he was there for almost four years and could read and write music but because he came to know both free people of color in the colony and enslaved people, including a young woman named Joanna, with whom he had a relationship and, eventually, a child.[2] Had he not learned Sranan Tongo to speak with Joanna or gotten to know her family members in Paramaribo and on plantations, he might not have been able to provide the insights he did.

Stedman thought the vocal music he heard was "melodious, but without time," though, meaning that it didn't necessarily keep a steady rhythm. He imagined it like a priest singing to a congregation, which could be like the *Sursum Corda* of a Catholic or Lutheran church, where the priest invites people to lift their hearts to God and the congregation responds. In that case, the phrases are the same each time, and the congregation knows what to sing back. In Suriname, Stedman noted that the lead singer pronounces "a sentence extempore, which he next hums or whistles, and then all the others repeat the same chorus," meaning that the leader can improvise and the singers can learn the song as they go, creating the call-and-response of the vocal melody.[3]

This did not mean that all the music Stedman heard played by people of African descent was "without time." On plantations Stedman sees dances where the music uses "full, or half measure, but never triple time," likely meaning 4/4 or 2/4 time but not 3/4 or 6/8 time. Here, the men and women "always [danced] in couples, the men figuring and footing, while the women turn round like a top, and their petticoats expand like a circle, which they call *waey cotto*," he writes.[4] Stedman doesn't attribute this to a particular group of enslaved people, so it was likely a creolized Afro-Surinamese dance.

This contrasts with a dance Stedman saw on another plantation that he calls "Loango-dancing." *Loango* is a term that Stedman uses for people he perceives to be from the Loango-Angola Central African coast. In this dance, men and women know the movements well from "constant practice," and they dance to a drum and the "clapping of hands." Stedman thinks it is "more like a play, divided into so many acts, which lasts hours together," and that the dancers eventually enter something like an ecstatic trance, with "their passions wound up to such a degree that nature being overcome, they are ready to drop into convulsions."[5]

In Suriname's only town of Paramaribo, Stedman relates that he was "present

"A Black Soldier's Song." The handwritten transcription in John Gabriel Stedman's manuscript dated 1790 of the song an enslaved ranger might sing before leaving for battle. James Ford Bell Library, University of Minnesota Libraries, Minneapolis.

Danse de Nègres (Black Dance), an engraving of men and women dancing to a drum and tambourine. In Moreau de Saint-Méry, Ponce, and Phelipeau, *Recueil de vues des lieux principaux de la colonie françoise de Saint-Domingue* (1791). This image is a copy of a 1779 engraving by Agostino Brunias titled *A Negroes Dance in the Island of Dominica*. James Ford Bell Library, University of Minnesota Libraries, Minneapolis.

at a Mulatto ball" with free people of color, "where the music, the lights, the country dances, the supper, and above all the dresses were so superb, and their behavior so decent and genteel that the *tout ensemble* might serve as a model for decorum and etiquette to the more fair and polished inhabitants," suggesting that free people of color had the same customs as (and better manners than) white inhabitants in Suriname.[6]

Stedman also hears of the *winty play* among the Maroons, which is part of the Winti religious practice, although Stedman did not know that. During this dance, women dance and whirl round "in the middle of the audience" until they collapse. This dance, Stedman hears, is dangerous because those who participate "are often told to murder their masters or desert into the woods," and so it was banned by the government. Bans don't manage to stop enslaved or free people of African descent from dancing or religious practices, and the *winty play* "is often put in execution in private spaces and is very common among the Auka and Saramake [Aluku and Saamaka Maroons]," Stedman writes.[7]

Even if Stedman could find a European analogy for the type of call-and-response singing he heard, his transcription of "A Black Soldier's Song" shows how hard it could be to put African-derived music into standard notation. Stedman does not add a time signature and does not divide the notes into measures, showing he really believes it to be without time. Perhaps the singer could choose to hold some of the quarter and half notes longer, if they wanted to.

A BLACK SOLDIER'S SONG

TRANSCRIPTION

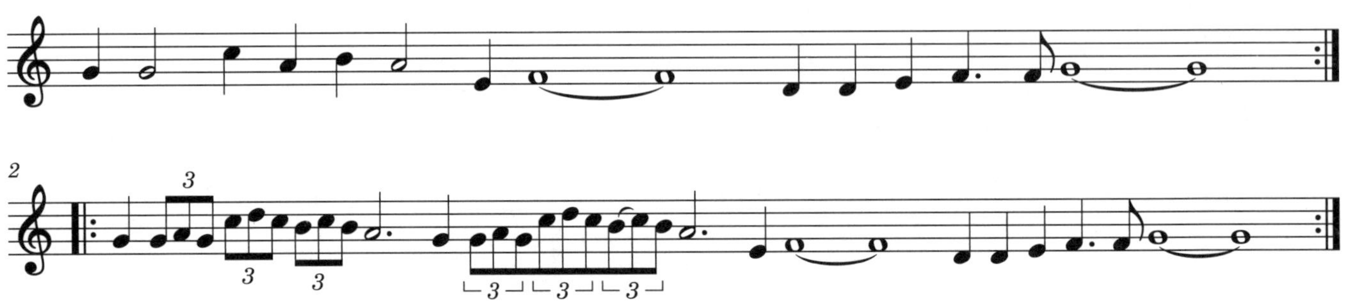

TABLATURE

cFCEG (As played by Rhiannon Giddens)*
gCGBD (Alternate modern tuning)

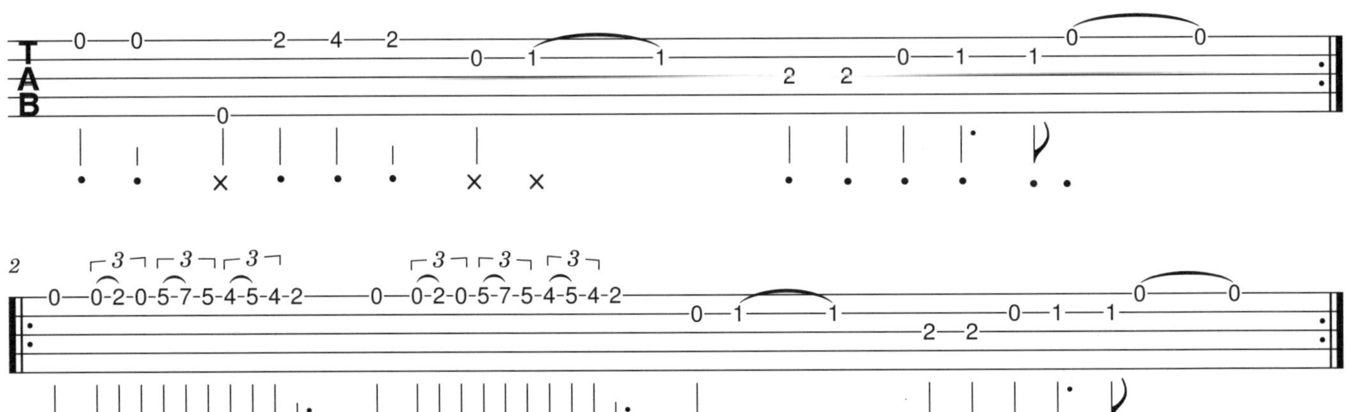

CHAPTER

Calemba and The Colymba

JAMAICA, 1770S

LATE ONE night in 1773, George and Lincoln were sitting in a cabin in Jamaica, George "playing upon the Banjar."[1] George and Lincoln were both enslaved, and according to a law that the government passed after the uprising of 1760 that became known as Tacky's Revolt, enslaved people were not supposed to be gathering or engaging in the African-derived spiritual practice called Obeah.[2] Did George and Lincoln know about the law? Probably, but they chose to meet and make music anyway. When Lincoln's enslaver found them, he destroyed the banjo. The enslaver might have destroyed the banjo because of its association with Obeah and spiritual practices.[3]

Lincoln's brutal owner recorded the destruction of the banjo in his diary but made no mention of the music George played. Around this same time, though, an unknown person did write down eleven pieces of music played and sung by enslaved people in Jamaica.[4] These "Jamaican Airs" included the pieces "Calemba" and "The Colymba."

The names "Calemba" and "The Colymba" are likely both derived from the Calinda dance, which also appears spelled as *kalinda*, *kalenda*, and *calendoe*. Governments banned Calinda dances because like Obeah and other gatherings, the dances could be used as an opportunity for insurrection. Even though these two songs have similar names, the transcriber places them in two separate categories. "Calemba" is one of five "Tunes in General Use," while "The Colymba" is "African Music," although the transcriber may have not had familiarity with actual music from Africa. As percussionist and composer Julian Gerstin points out, descriptions of the Calinda "vary greatly" in historical accounts, from line dances to stick fighting.[5] The similar name may suggest that the songs may have had a similar origin point in an older dance or that Calinda was a broader category than European observers understood.

The "African Music" section begins with the note "Negroe ~~Dances~~ songs which are likewise Dances" and includes "The Colymba" and "The Myal." Myal, like Obeah, served as a spiritual practice for people of African descent in Jamaica. Historian Mary Turner explains that the Obeah and Myal men or women collected the spirit world, and literary historians Margarite Fernandez Olmos and Lizabeth Paravisini-Gebert explain that Myal involved dancing in a way that may have induce a hypnotic trance, and in a ritual like Haitian Vodou, it may have allowed spirits to enter a dancer.[6]

"The Colymba" is in 2/4 time and F major. Jamaican plantation owner and enslaver Bryan Edwards thought that the banjo could produce only "four notes," which would have made it unsuitable for most of the written melodies of the "Jamaican Airs."[7] However, "The Colymba" can be played on a four-string gourd- or calabash-bodied banjo and, as an African dance tune, would have been suited for the banjo. Visiting Antigua in the late 1780s, cartographer John Luffman believed

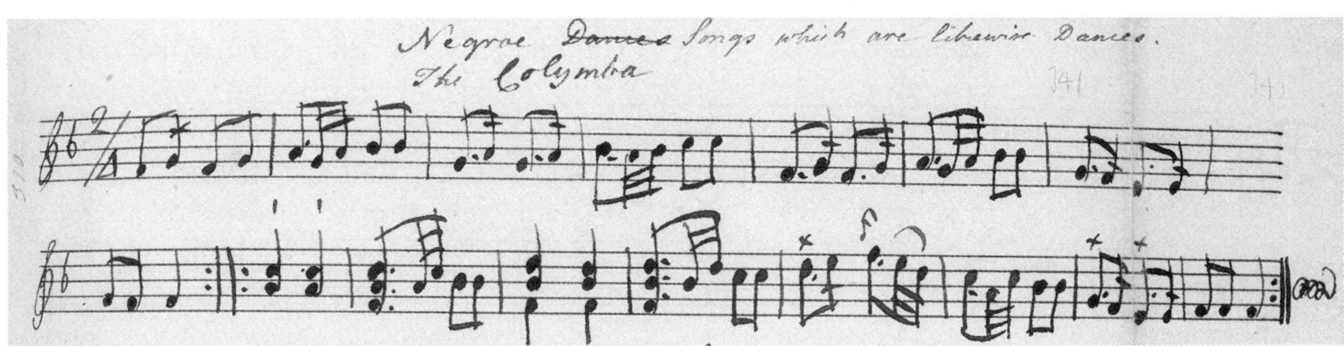

TOP "Calemba," a transcription of a "Jamaican Air" in "general use." Some of the tunes in the collection also have a guitar part written out. Courtesy of Devin Leigh. Add. MS 12405, fols. 335r–341v, C. E. Long Papers, British Library Collection, London.

BOTTOM "The Colymba," a piece of "African Music" from Jamaica. Eleven total songs were transcribed by an unknown white enslaver before 1776. Courtesy of Devin Leigh. Add. MS 12405, fols. 335r–341v, C. E. Long Papers, British Library Collection, London.

that enslaved people played "principally their own country tunes" (meaning "African" songs) on the banjo and wrote that he did not "remember ever to have heard any thing like European numbers from its touch."[8]

The "Tunes in General Use" were popular songs in Jamaica at the time and span dance songs and work songs. "Calemba" is in G major and 4/4 time, with a tempo of "Andante Allegro" and unsyncopated rhythm. The even meter would make it appropriate for a country dance, where couples dance set figures. The Yoruba of people of present-day Nigeria and Benin have a religious dance where partners form a circle that historian Monica Schuler calls a country dance, but these dances would have also been influenced by English country dances.[9] The transcriber of the songs notes that Black musicians play the violin with "Country Dances," furthering the connection to a European tradition.[10]

What's clear from the "Jamaican Airs" is that even though two songs are designated as "African," the creolization between different African and European cultures was fully underway in the Americas.

CALEMBA

TRANSCRIPTION

TABLATURE

cFCEG (As played by Rhiannon Giddens)
gCGBD (Alternate modern tuning)*

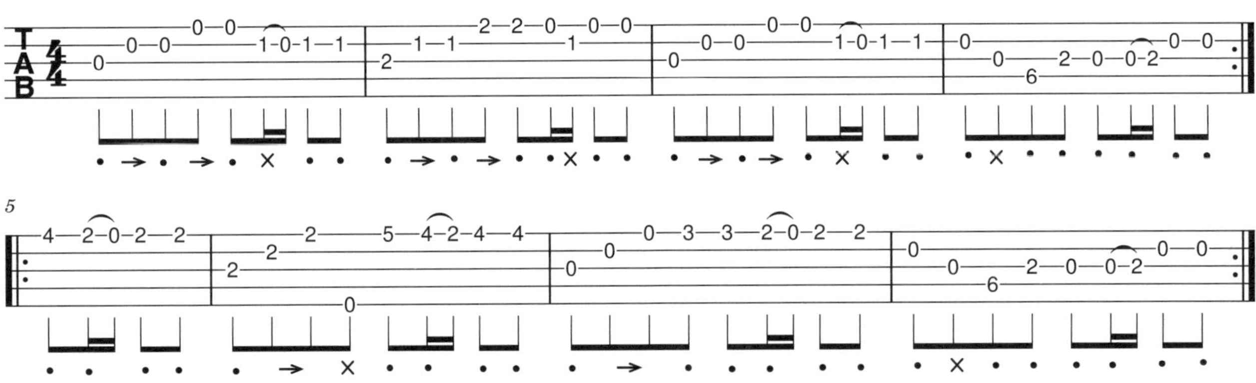

THE COLYMBA

TRANSCRIPTION

cFCEG (As played by Rhiannon Giddens)*
gCGBD (Alternate modern tuning)

TABLATURE

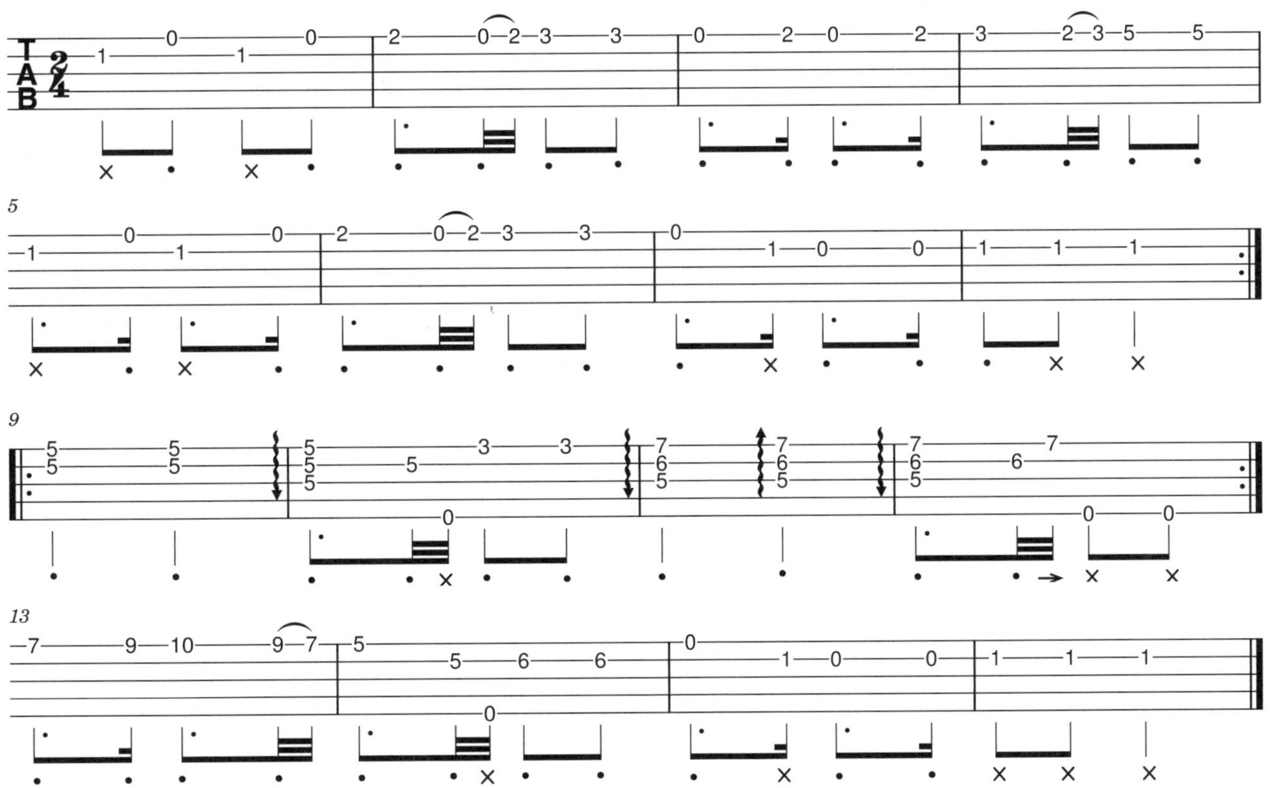

Five people dancing in a circle to a tambourine and perhaps a chorus, a detail from *Recueil de vues des lieux principaux de la colonie française de Saint-Domingue*, 1791. James Ford Bell Library, University of Minnesota Libraries, Minneapolis.

CHAPTER

Pompey Ran Away

VIRGINIA, 1782

"POMPEY RAN AWAY" is one of the better-known tunes in this collection, with recorded versions and the transcription easily available with a quick Internet search. Dena Epstein included the piece in her groundbreaking book *Sinful Tunes and Spirituals*, and eager musicians and scholars (ourselves included) have taken the subtitle "Negroe Jig" mainly at face value. Although many tunes we're publishing here still hold their secrets, none is harder to explore and explain than "Pompey Ran Away."

We know little about where the tune came from, who played it, why it was collected, and, honestly, if it is definitely part of the Black music tradition. The tune first appears in the historical record in *A Selection of Scotch, English, Irish, and Foreign Airs, Adapted to the Fife, Violin, or German-Flute*, printed and sold in 1782 by Glasgow, Scotland, music seller James Aird.[1] Aird compiled these pieces from "pre-existing publications," although no earlier transcription of "Pompey Ran Away" has been found.[2] Aird must have had North American sources for the music, since the tunes "Old Plantation Girls" and "Sam Jones" in the collection are designated as "Virginian." People have assumed that "Pompey Ran Away" must also be from Virginia (and we're also designating it as such), but Aird does not give the song a geographical appellation.

The subtitle "Negroe Jig" seems as if it should be a designation of who played the song (Black people) and the style of song (a fast dance tune called a jig). The tunes in this book were essentially collected for white audiences and underwent a process of transmission to standard notation, and we believe that they at least have an original Black source. No one has found such record for "Pompey Ran Away." Musicologist Paul F. Wells points out that the subtitle could then mean the transcriber was writing a tune in the style of a "Negroe Jig," whatever that meant to them. Perhaps the composer thought that the melody sounded African American because of the rhythms or phrasing

A woman dancing to a Black violinist (perhaps her dance instructor) in P. J. Benoit's *Voyage à Suriname* (1839). She is on her toes with her legs straight and torso upright in what scholar Christopher J. Smith terms "Anglo-European body aesthetics," suggesting that she is dancing to "European" rather than "African" music. It was also very common for women, especially enslaved women, to not wear tops before emancipation in Suriname. Internet Archive.

or notes. Wells believes that the repetition of the melodic motif in the first and second parts of the tune and the melody's limit within an octave are characteristic of "African melodic practice."[3] The tune could have come from the Black tradition or been composed by a Black musician.

As a jig, "Pompey Ran Away" would have been a dance tune, and in North America, the designation as a jig would have actually connected the song to the Black tradition more strongly. In the 1770s, a "Reverend Gentleman" from Virginia reported that after an evening of country dances, white attendees danced jigs, "a practice originally borrowed" from Black Americans.[4] In Alexandria, Virginia, British visitor to the colonies Nicholas Cresswell wrote that between country dances, white people danced "everlasting jigs" to a "Negro tune."[5] These jigs are understood as being influenced by or taken from the African American musical tradition.

"Pompey Ran Away" is atypical of jigs because jig are typically in 6/8 time: the two other jigs in Aird's collection are in 6/8 time, but "Pompey Ran Away" is in 3/4 time. This is an unusual choice for the transcriber because 3/4 is usually reserved for waltzes. However, unlike a waltz, in which there is a stress only on the first beat, "Pompey Ran Away" feels as if it wants to be in 6/8, with a large stress on the first beat and a lesser stress on the fourth.

In the banjo tab, Rhiannon has chosen to notate chords for the first beats of measures one and three. This isn't present in the original treble-clef notation (and would be impossible on fife or German flute), but it adds flair and just sounds nice.

Although there had been a voyeurism of Black American music for more than 100 years, the 1780s seem to be a time when people of European descent in the Americas begin to have a desire to emulate and participate in that Black music. We see this desire with "Pompey Ran Away," which, if it is a Virginia tune, amazingly appears across an ocean in a published song collection. We see it also in other transcriptions made in the Americas and descriptions of white music-making across the Americas, including in "Black Dance" (Piece 6) and "Congo" (Piece 7).

POMPEY RAN AWAY

TRANSCRIPTION

cFCEG (As played by Rhiannon Giddens)
gCGBD (Alternate modern tuning)
dGDF♯A (To play with transcription)

TABLATURE

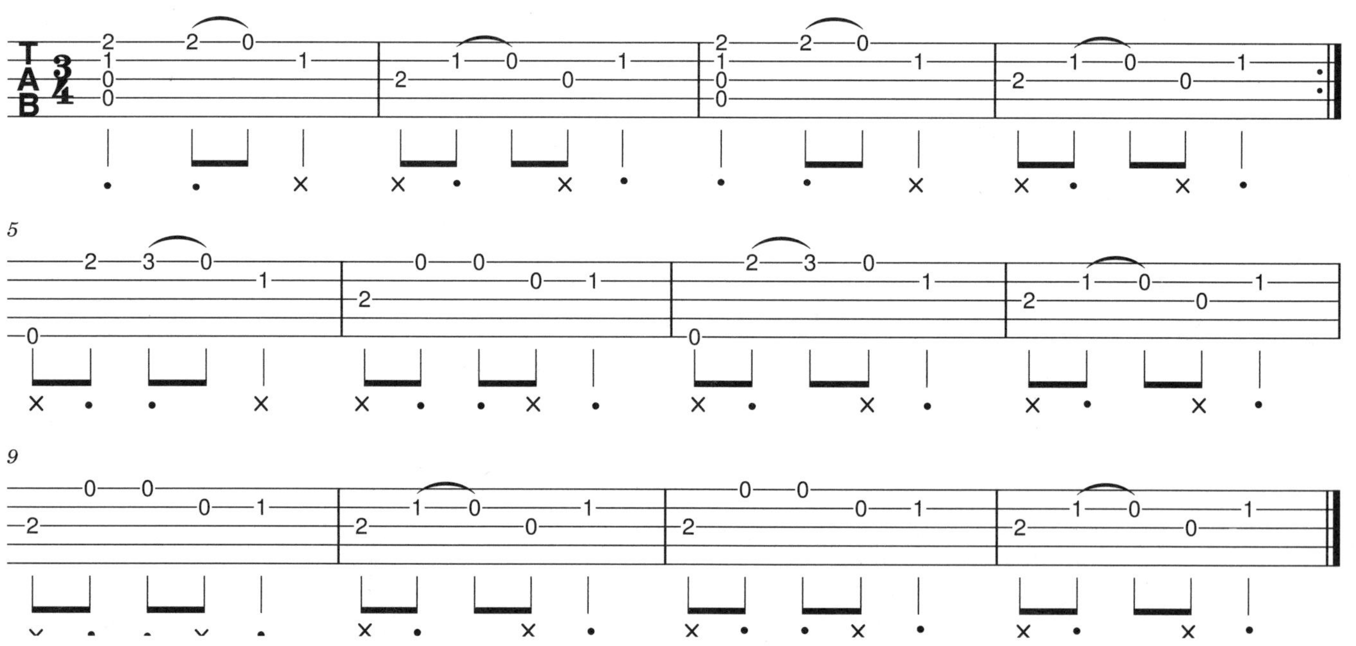

CHAPTER

Black Dance

SAINT-BARTHÉLEMY, 1788

On the first Friday following Dr. Christopher Carlander's arrival from Sweden on the island of Saint-Barthélemy in 1788, he saw a captain named Skånberg and a woman he called Queen Christina, likely a woman of color, with a group of people dancing "a rather ridiculous contradance."[1] In this part of Carlander's diary, he didn't explain what he found ridiculous. Perhaps he didn't expect to see Black and white people dancing together; or maybe these were unlike the dances he was familiar with in Sweden, where people of his class were more likely to emulate French court dancing than English country dances; or possibly he found it amusing that Queen Christina and other Black people were imitating country dances. One thing became clear to Carlander during his stay: dancing was a common occurrence on Saint-Barthélemy, and the lines between Black and white musical culture were blurrier than someone in Europe might imagine.

Like Hans Sloane in Jamaica, Carlander had journeyed to the Caribbean to serve as a doctor but also took the opportunity to collect natural history specimens and provide a report on the formerly French, now Swedish, colony. In his diary and then in a more formal accounting of Saint-Barthélemy, Carlander wrote about music and dance on the island. He took down musical notation of three songs he heard and the dance steps that went along with them, including a tune called "Black Dance."

All three songs were different from what Carlander had heard in Sweden, and he thought that this was "Black music," although two of the songs were well known to dancers and musicians in the United States. "College Hornpipe," also known as "Sailor's Hornpipe" (also known as the lead-in to the *Popeye the Sailor* theme), and "Rodney's March" both appear in American handwritten music manuscripts and published songbooks from the 1780s and 1790s.[2]

Carlander didn't explicitly say who danced each of these songs, although he did note in his diary that one night he danced "a good College Hornpipe."

Saint-Barthélemy was unusual for the Caribbean because drought conditions made large scale plantations unsustainable. Almost everyone lived in the port town of Gustavia, and in 1788, there were about 200 enslaved people on the island and some free people of color. Most of the inhabitants, however, were of European descent—English, French, and Swedish, along with Dutch, Danish, American, Spanish, and German.[3]

Carlander wrote about the music and dancing of the various groups on the island. When he first arrived, Carlander thought everything on the island was beautiful "except the Blacks and their singing," but again, he didn't expand on exactly what it was he objected to.[4] He, like soldier John Gabriel Stedman, might have been making a judgment specifically about people who were carrying on perceived African traditions. The enslaved people gathered on Saturday and Sunday afternoons, Carlander wrote. By law, they were allowed to dance only until 8:00 p.m. Carlander writes that they danced outside "in their own manner, two and two," perhaps suggesting that he did not recognize any figures or formal dance steps. The enslaved people on the island were mostly born in the Caribbean, but some had also been taken from Africa, so "in their own manner" could have meant that he perceived the dances to be African or Afro-Caribbean.[5] "The music is made up of two drums, open on one side and hit with the hands; a woman who sings and hits a rattle with her hand; and the others clap their hands and make a strong chorus with the solo voice," Carlander wrote, adding that those who dance are careful and serious.[6]

A few months into his sojourn, Carlander seemed to gain more of an appreciation for the music, since it was Black music, he said, that was played for the dances for Europeans. "Here there is nothing other than Black music, including some from St. Martin, that is sometimes a little motley and unusual, but nevertheless works," he wrote.[7] For "Black Dance," Carlander wrote out specific dance figures, suggesting that the piece was not a dance done by the enslaved people, although the musicians would have been of African descent. During the first two figures of "Black Dance," each pair makes a half *ronde*, which would mean joining hands and walking in a circle figure. Then, the first couple walks to the second couple, and the first gentleman picks up the partner of the second couple. Although the handwriting is hard to decipher, it then seems as though during the fourth and fifth figures, the new partner repeats the figure and goes forward and back. On the sixth figure, the couple promenades, cuts (walks away from each other), takes each other up again, and then goes behind and around their partner. The dance directions suggest that this was not a jig, as in the subtitle of "Pompey Ran Away" (Piece 5), but still something that a European observer considered "Black" and perhaps more like the dance that might have accompanied "Calemba" (Piece 4a) in Jamaica.

This set dancing was popular in Saint-Barthélemy. "Quadrilles are called French dances, which are not requested often; Minuets are danced at length by Englishmen and [are made fun of by the French].—The Congo minuet is a new style, but not so bad," Carlander reported.[8] The Creoles (in this case meaning people of European descent born in the Caribbean) jump during their line dances, Carlander wrote, and ask for reprises. "The

Christopher Carlander's transcriptions of music in Saint-Barthélemy. The songs are "Rodney's Marche" (or "Rodney's March," also known as "Lord Cornwallis") with dance steps; "College Hornpipe" (also known as "Sailor's Hornpipe"); and "Black Dance." Courtesy of Fredrik Thomasson, document 1, Chr. Carlander Collection, Svenska Läkaresällskapet, Riksarkivet (Swedish National Archives), Stockholm.

jumping is so regular that they never lose the beat." In a Swedish dance book from the same time, any jumps or hops were supposed to be small.[9]

The people Carlander perceives to be of mixed European and African descent and the "higher class Blacks" receive permission from the governor for their dances, Carlander wrote, since free people of color were not allowed to assemble without permission.[10] Sweden had adapted the French Code Noir, a system of laws that governed the behavior of enslaved and free Black people, as well as how white people were supposed to interact with people of African descent. However, with permission, free people of color danced "their minuets and contradances, and often better than the above-mentioned whites."[11] This was similar to how John Gabriel Stedman described dances in Suriname, and thirty-five years later a visitor to Jamaica also wrote that at a ball hosted by a free woman of color, "dancers, male and female, acquitted themselves famously well, and performed country-dances and quadrilles quite as well, if not better, than I had ever seen at a country ball in England." The band for this Jamaican dance—"three fiddles, a pipe and tambor, and a triangle"—is almost the same as the band Carlander describes for white dances in Saint-Barthélemy: three violinists, two drummers, and a person playing percussion on a fire tong in lieu of a triangle.[12]

"Black Dance" is in G major and 2/4 time and, except for a combination of two sixteenth notes followed by an eighth note, is straight and unsyncopated. There are two main parts of four measures each, which are

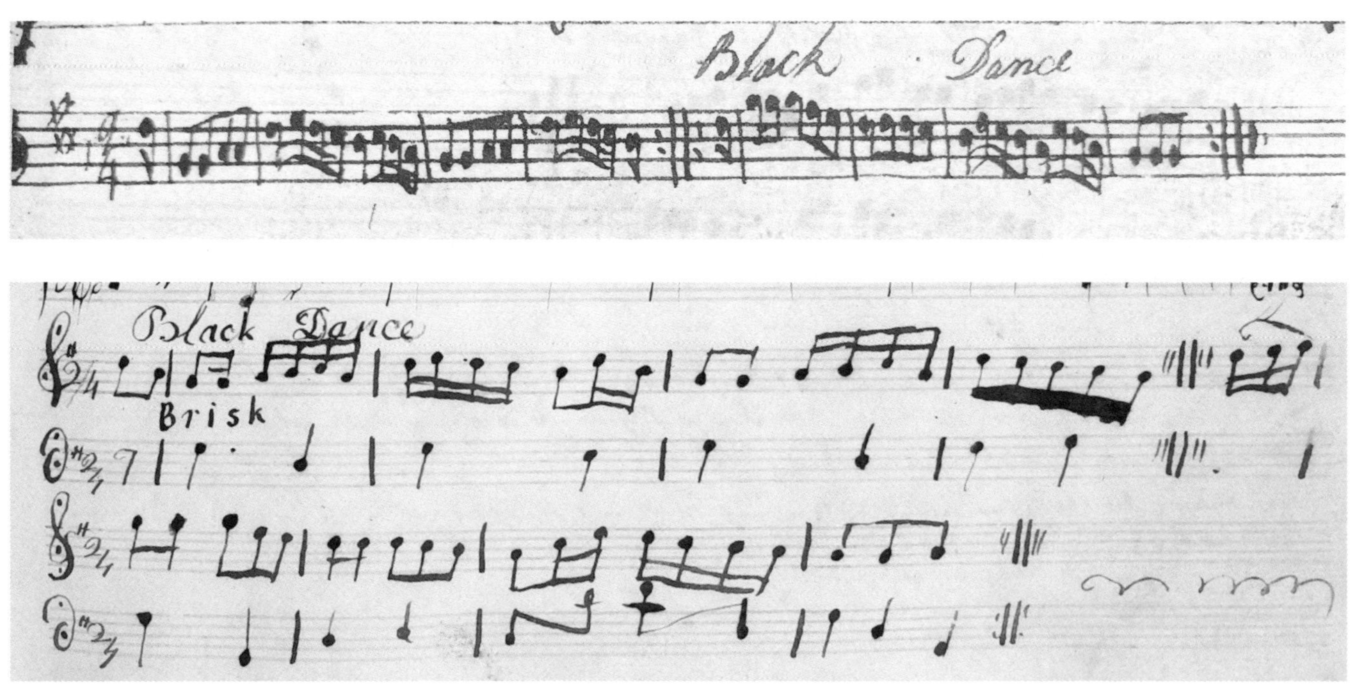

TOP "Black Dance" transcribed in Abel Shattuck's music manuscript, ca. 1801. Library of Congress, Washington, DC.

BOTTOM "Black Dance" in Elizabeth Van Rensselaer's music book, ca. 1782. The three transcriptions of "Black Dance" are slightly different, but all seem to be essentially the same tune. Courtesy of Watkinson Library, Trinity College, Hartford, Connecticut.

to be repeated, and the final four measures have the words "Black variation on the last reprise" above them.

The title alone is intriguing, and tunes with the title "Black Dance" also appear in music manuscripts and published songbooks in the last two decades of the eighteenth century and into the nineteenth century.

The earliest known "Black Dance" is in a handwritten manuscript of 1782 compiled by Elizabeth Sanders Van Rensselaer. Van Rensselaer was a descendant of a founder of the Dutch West India Company (which founded and owned part of Suriname), and her father, Philip, owned a woman named Bet, who was accused of setting a destructive fire in Albany with an enslaved man named Pompey in 1793.[13] During Van Rensselaer's lifetime, Albany was also home to Pinkster festivities. The Black celebration, which coincided with the Christian Pentecost holiday, brought music, dancing, a procession, and vendors selling food and drink to a hill overlooking the city. The celebration was eventually banned because that was easier than trying to keep white residents from attending the Black celebration.[14] The handwritten book where Van Rensselaer copied down "Black Dance" acted like the recording device a musician today might bring to a jam. She would have written down new or unfamiliar songs she wished to learn and play again. Although some of such surviving manuscripts give attribution, we don't know where Van Rensselaer heard "Black Dance."

Like Carlander's, Van Renssalaer's "Black Dance" is in G major and 2/4 time. Unlike Carlander's, though, it has a three-against-two rhythm with triplets in the second part, giving it syncopation. A transcription of "Black Dance" in Abel Shattuck's handwritten music book of 1801 also has triplets in the second part, but it has slight differences from Van Rensselaer's, showing again how a song transforms over time and space.

BLACK DANCE

TRANSCRIPTION

TABLATURE

cGCEG (As played by Rhiannon Giddens)
gDGBD (Alternate modern tuning)*

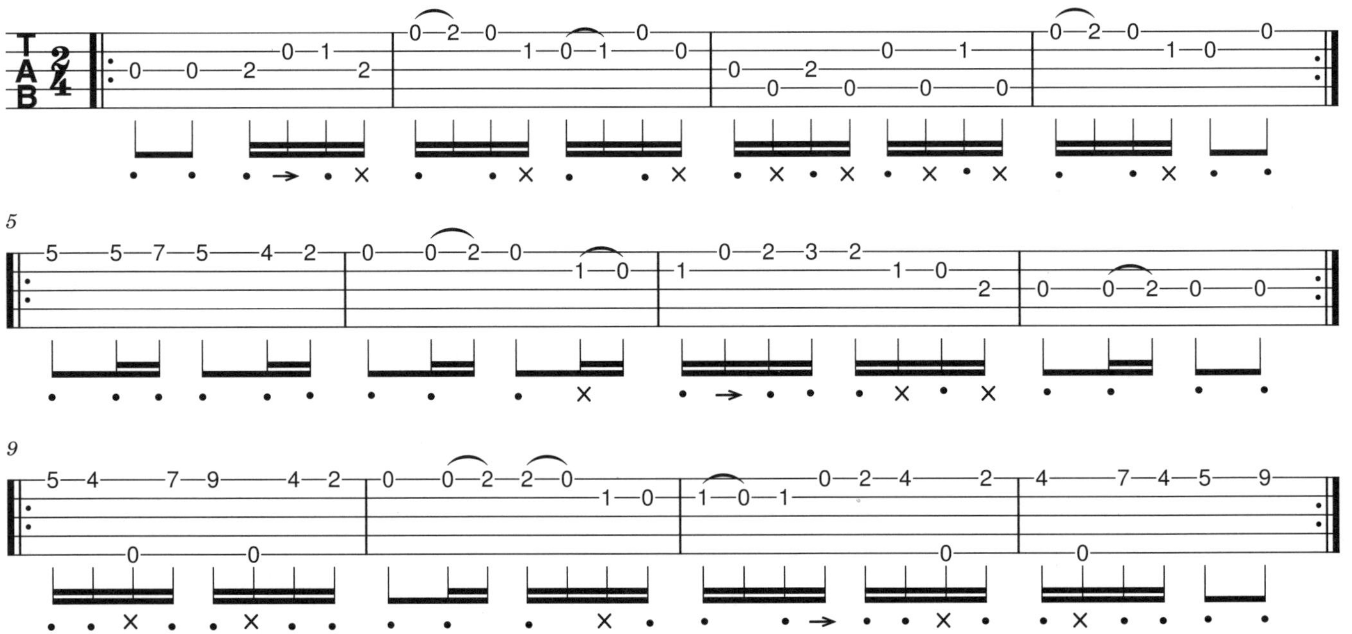

CHAPTER

Congo

VIRGINIA, CA. 1790

In the handwritten music manuscript of the Bolling family, there is a piece of music as intriguing and mysterious as "Pompey Ran Away" (Piece 5) and "Black Dance" (Piece 6) titled simply "Congo" and in 6/8 time (like a jig). The history behind the piece requires a triangulation among what we know about the Bolling family's life in central Virginia, dance and music at the time, and what we can infer from other mentions of Congo dances.

Although the Bolling family left this rare music manuscript, most of the papers that remain from the family concern money: the expenses of Lenaeus Bolling's widowed mother, the income from tobacco and other crops, and property records. But because the family's property also included human beings, we can learn something about the enslaved people the Bollings owned and knew. Prince and Isaac were two enslaved men that the Bollings trusted enough to carry mail between family members in Buckingham County, Virginia. An enslaved man and wife named Tim and Betty were born two years after the American Revolution and went on to have six children: Daniel, Richard, Henry, King, Joycy, and Kitt. When an enslaved man named Jacob got sick, the overseer put him under the care of an enslaved Black doctor.[1] According to family lore, Lenaeus fathered at least one enslaved child, future Virginia House of Delegates member Samuel P. Bolling.[2]

The Bolling family was also musical. Lenaeus (also spelled Linnaeus) and his father were musicians and even composed some of the pieces in the manuscript. Lenaeus's brother Powhatan (named after the tribe of their fourth great-grandmother Pocahontas) was an "ardent violinist" and "somewhat eccentric."[3] It isn't impossible to imagine that an enslaved fiddler played for the Bolling family's dances or that Lenaeus or Powhatan had musical exchanges with enslaved musicians. Around the same time, Thomas Jefferson's brother Randolph was known to go where enslaved people were playing music and dancing at Monticello, Jefferson's plantation outside Charlottesville, Virginia.[4]

In the historical record, there are essentially two styles of dances that are called Congo. The first was played for Black dancers by Black musicians and often called the Congo Dance, although like the Calinda (see "Calemba" and "The Colymba," chapter 4), it had multiple variations. In the late 1600s or early 1700s in Martinique, Father Jean-Baptiste Labat described a dance performed by people he believed to be from the Congo where male and female dancers stood in a circle and stomped their feet in a cadence, with someone telling a story and the chorus repeating a refrain. Between 1815 and 1825, Rev. Timothy Flint traveled the Mississippi River Valley and described a "great Congo-dance" in New Orleans and the surrounding area. He described a procession of people following a king with "a series of oblong, gilt-paper boxes on his head, tapering upwards, like a pyramid," similar to Junkanoo parades in North Carolina and the

"Congo." Hubard Family Papers, University of North Carolina Southern Folklife Collection, Wilson Library, University of North Carolina at Chapel Hill.

Caribbean.[5] Around the same time, another European observer wrote that in Louisiana and Mississippi, enslaved people danced "the Congo dance" on Sundays "for several hours during the afternoon" to the sound of a drum and singing.[6] In 1843, the New Orleans *Times Picayune* reported on "The Congo Dance," where one man and two women danced to the sound of "a long-necked banjo," someone playing a donkey jawbone with a key, and a drum made of a "butter firkin." The women moved "their feet rapidly, but still with the least possible visible motion," and the man had on "a pair of leather knee caps from which were suspended a quantity of metal nails," which added to the percussion.[7] Some or all of these dances may be related to the Congo sect (or "nation") of Vodou, which is still practiced today. In Haiti, a dancer of this sect "moves his feet imperceptibly and gives small shakes to his shoulders while gently undulating his hips" and then turns round and round.[8] In the historic accounts, no observer described the music of any of these dances in detail, yet the brief descriptions don't seem to match the style of music in the Bolling manuscript.

The second Congo dance in the historic record had a European influence, yet the name "Congo" suggests that it had an African influence.[9] In Saint-Barthélemy in 1788, Dr. Christopher Carlander reported that "the Congo minuet is a new style, but not so bad."[10] A minuet is a moderate-tempo French dance in 3/4 time with A and B parts that each repeat once (AABB) but was not just a dance for Europeans or people of European descent. However, the Bolling manuscript "Congo" is in 6/8 time and has three parts, making it unlike minuets of the eighteenth century. Around the turn of the nineteenth century, Englishman John Davis wrote a fictionalized memoir about his time in Virginia in which an enslaved man named Dick recounts that his enslaver "could shake a desperate foot at the fiddle; there was nobody that could face him at a Congo Minuet."[11] In a letter to University of North Carolina president Joseph Caldwell in 1797, Richard Dobbs Spaight writes that he believes the Congo to

He does not undertake to teach the english dances but, the minuet, & french dances such as Cotillions Congos &c. &c. his terms are two Dollars pr. month for which he teaches three afternoons in each week. General Davie supposes he may get between

Extract from a 1797 letter from North Carolina governor Richard Dobbs Spaight to University of North Carolina president Joseph Caldwell introducing Mr. Perrin, the French dance master. Some scholars believe that Mr. Perrin was a refugee from the Haitian Revolution. University of North Carolina Papers, no. 40005, University Archives, Wilson Library, University of North Carolina at Chapel Hill.

be a French dance. He states that the French dance master Mr. Perrin "does not undertake to teach the english dances but, the minuet, + french dances such as cotillions, congos, etc. etc."[12] Instructions for the "Congo Minuet" appear in an American dance instructor of 1802 with the note that the time (tempo) "must be played quick and spirited."[13] This does not mean that only people of European descent danced minuets. As early as the 1690s, Father Jean-Baptiste Labat wrote that he tried to teach enslaved people the minuet so they would stop dancing the Calinda. Observers later wrote about people of African descent dancing minuets in 1770s Suriname, 1780s Saint-Domingue, and early 1800s Berbice, and African-born composer Ignatius Sancho composed a minuet in the 1760s.[14] Some scholars have suggested that the Congo minuet originated in the French Caribbean, either as the Afro-Caribbean version of the French dance, or as a European or white imitation of the African Congo dances.[15]

Musical pieces including "Pompey Ran Away" (Piece 5), "Black Dance" (Piece 6), and "Congo" exist in a liminal space before the advent of Blackface Minstrelsy in the late 1820s, when we know how fascinated white audiences were by Black music. The titles of these three pieces directly reference Black culture, and yet we don't know whether they were composed by white folks in the imitation of Black music or came from Black musicians. We can imagine that they would be played for a Congo minuet or other dances that were a part of African American culture or for jigs in ballrooms that were danced by white people.

CONGO

TRANSCRIPTION

TABLATURE

cFCEG (As played by Rhiannon Giddens)
gCGBD (Alternate modern tuning)*

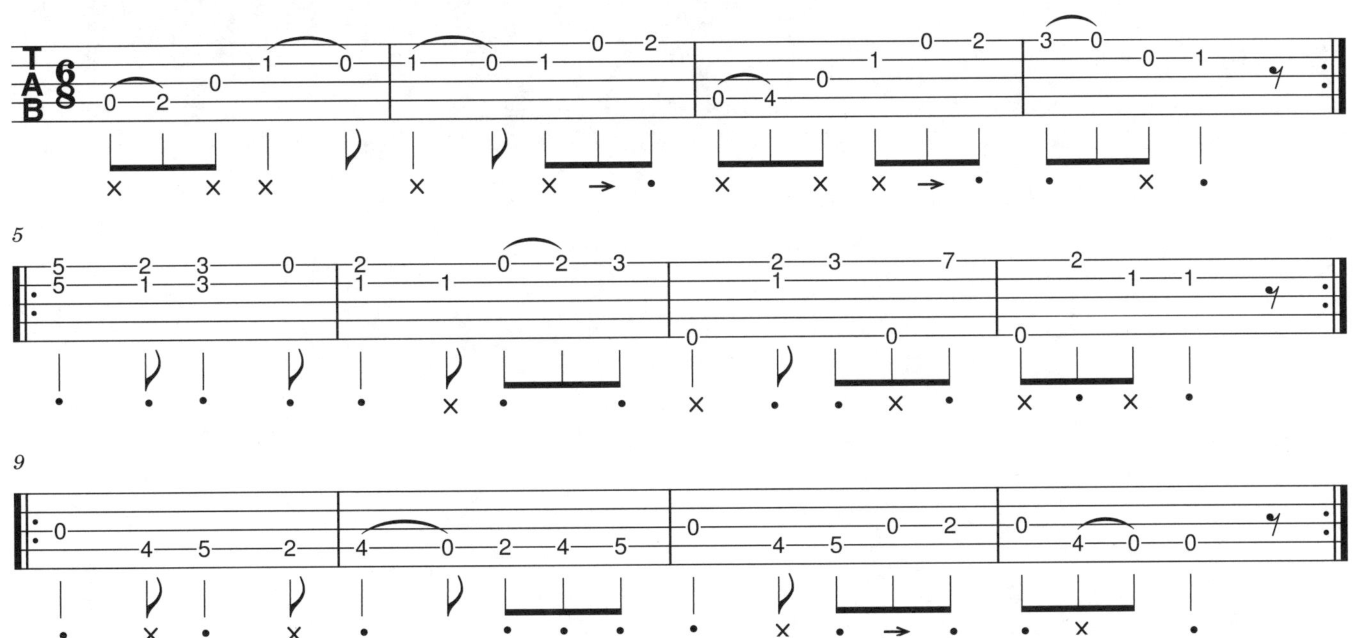

A Vodou dance at the burial ground outside of Cap-Français, Saint-Domingue, before the Haitian Revolution.

CHAPTER

Aia bombaia bombé

HAITI, 1814

As people of African descent in the Americas played and danced to secular music, they still also played and danced to religious music. These practices were a blend of African religions and could sometimes be disguised as or practiced in tandem with Christianity and included Vodou in Haiti, Winti in Suriname, Candomblé in Brazil, Santería in Cuba, Myal in Jamaica, and the shout and praise songs and dances in South Carolina and Georgia. Outsiders—especially people of European descent—didn't understand the ways in which music and dance could call on the power of gods and ancestors, and they therefore saw these practices as dangerous. In the 1810s, white Creole planter Drouin de Bercy heard the "Aia bombaia bombé" song as part of a Vodou "initiation ceremony . . . presided over by a *vaudou* 'king and queen.'"[1] He believed that the aim of the religion was to ruin and destroy white people, and the lyrics he wrote down spoke to that fear.

It wasn't wrong for de Bercy to see a connection between Vodou music and rebellion. The Haitian Revolution of 1791 began with a man named Boukman leading enslaved people "in a religious ceremony" that involved dancing.[2] More than fifty years earlier, on a Sunday in September 1739 in South Carolina, over sixty enslaved people started "dancing, singing and beating Drums" at the beginning of what would become known as the Stono Rebellion.[3] In Jamaica in 1760, a man named Tacky gathered a few supporters and was said to have been bound to them with an Obeah oath, and they went on to burn plantations and free enslaved people.[4] Even in Haiti after the revolution, Vodou dances were banned in 1796 and suppressed by the postrevolution Black military leader Henri Christophe.[5] And yet, de Bercy heard "Aia bombaia bombé" long after the revolution—proof that the bans did not stop religious music and dance.

De Bercy's book essentially advocated for the restoration of slavery and is filled with racist and stereotyped descriptions of Vodou. For that reason, some scholars have completely dismissed the lyrics he recorded. And yet, de Bercy's translation does show that he wanted the song to confirm the danger of Vodou for his readers. He states that the lyrics said, "We swear to destroy the whites and all that they possess, let us die rather than renounce this vow."[6]

Even with that consideration, the song isn't a complete invention. The first line is similar to the "Hi-a-bomba, bomba, bomba" lyrics that drummer Jackey Quakenboss sang in Albany during the Pinkster celebrations around the first decade of the 1800s.[7] The lyrics are also similar to ones that another white Creole heard in Haiti before the revolution: "Eh! Eh! Bomba, hen! Hen!," which scholars believe is in Kongo or Kikongo and references the Mbumba Kongo deity.[8] In the 1930s, Melville and Frances Herskovits heard a Winti dance in Suriname with the chorus, "Bumba-e, Kere Bumba-e," and although they didn't have a translation, the "Bomba or Boema" was a water god the song might be invoking.[9]

"Aia bombaia bombé" is in 2/4 time and G major. The major, rather than minor, key makes it different from the religious *Banja* and Winti songs of Suriname, "The Colymba" (Piece 4b) song from Jamaica, and many of the shout and praise songs in *Slave Songs of the United States* that we couldn't fit into this book. "Aia bombaia bombé" relies mostly on the pentatonic scale (GABDE), with a few F-sharps and Cs in passing, and overall there's a chant- or march-like feel to the song. We encourage readers to compare the original notation to our transcription of it. For example, we thought measures two, four, eight, twelve, and fourteen looked more like a quarter note followed by an eighth note rest, although it also resembles a dotted quarter note. The note stems and beams in measure ten of the original transcription are askew because of how the music was printed.

(178)

« A ia bombaia bombé, lamma samana quana, é van » vanta, vana docki, qui signifient, nous jurons de dé- » truire les blancs et tout ce qu'ils possèdent, mourrons » plutôt que d'y renoncer. »

Après le serment, les hommes et les femmes se mettent à danser tout nuds, et à boire du tafia. La salle n'offre plus ensuite qu'une orgie indécente, dans laquelle les deux sexes se trouvent enlacés dans les bras les uns des autres.

Musique des paroles ci-dessus.

FIN.

Drouin de Bercy's printed version of "Aia bombaia bombé." New York Public Library Collections, New York.

The D note on beat one, which looks like a quarter note in the original transcription, is most likely meant to be an eighth note followed by two sixteenth notes.

Although secular set dances and music for Black jigs were increasing in visibility and popularity in the early 1800s, Black musicians and dancers were still playing religious music associated with such African diasporic religions as Vodou, Winti, and Myal and, increasingly, with Christianity.

AIA BOMBAIA BOMBÉ

TRANSCRIPTION

AIA BOMBAIA BOMBÉ

cFCEG (As played by Rhiannon Giddens)
gCGBD (Alternate modern tuning)
dGDF♯A (To play with transcription)

TABLATURE

CHAPTER

Roaring River

LOUISIANA, 1840S

"ALAS! Had it not been for my beloved violin, I scarcely can conceive how I could have endured the long years of my bondage," Solomon Northup wrote in his memoir *Twelve Years a Slave*.[1] He was born free in New York and had played violin since he was a child, and in 1841, two men offered him a job playing for a circus. After he arrived in Washington, DC, he was drugged, woke up in chains, and then sold into slavery. Northrup's memoir gives insight into the life of an enslaved Black fiddler as no other source does, and he provided one of the few tunes from before US Emancipation of Black vernacular music: "Roaring River."

Music was a part of the joy and sorrow that Northup experienced as an enslaved man. When he thought of what had happened—how he had been taken and didn't know when he would see his wife and children again—his fiddle "would sing me a song a peace," he wrote. When he arrived in New Orleans, people were "paraded and made to dance" before being sold, and he played the fiddle for the spectacle.[2] Later, one of Northrup's enslavers would regularly force the enslaved people he owned to assemble "in the large room of the great house. . . . [And] no matter how worn out and tired we were, there must be a general dance" for the enslaver's amusement. He might beat them if they didn't dance to Northrup's "marvelous quick-stepping tune."[3]

Northup was also asked to play at other plantations, and even if his enslaver took his earnings, he might be able to pocket the tips. His fiddle playing "introduced me to great houses—relieved me of many days' labor in the field—supplied me with conveniences for my cabin—with pipes and tobacco, and extra pair of shoes, and oftentimes led me away from the presence of a hard master, to witness scenes of jollity and mirth." This travel also meant that enslaved musicians were in a better position to take their own freedom. They might have extra money and often had clothing that would both make their appearance suitable to play for an audience and perhaps look like free men. In fact, the fiddle was the most common instrument mentioned in eighteenth-century runaway ads, with more than eight in ten enslaved musicians playing the fiddle.[4]

As a musician, Northrup also offered insight into the musical lives of the people he came to know in Bayou Bœuf, about fifty miles outside of New Orleans. As many others had observed, Northrup wrote that the only time off they received was during Christmas. "It is the custom for one planter to give a 'Christmas supper,'" where up to 500 enslaved people might gather. Everyone wore their best outfits, and red was an especially popular color, perhaps stemming from traditions of Kongo royalty wearing red or the color red bringing good luck and driving away evil spirits.[5] People ate and "fun and merriment flow[ed] on," until the dance. Northrup's job was always "to play on the violin," and while some "could thumb the banjo with dexterity," he was the master fiddler.

The dances were not "slow-winding cotillions" but "rampant and unrestrained" dances. During one Christmas dance, Miss Lively and Mr. Sam danced together, until Sam got exhausted and another man, Pete Marshall, took his place "with might and main, leaped and shuffled and threw himself into every conceivable shape" to impress Miss Lively.[6] The men and women danced in pairs, reminiscent of the "Congo Dance" described in 1843 in New Orleans, rather than in sets as they might in a more European contra, square, or line dance.[7]

During a Christmas party that Miss Mary McCoy provided for enslaved people, Northrup wrote that he "struck up a lively air; while some joined in a nimble reel, others patted and sang their simple but melodious songs, filling the great room with music mingled with the sound of human voices and the clatter of many feet."[8] A reel would be more like the set dances and cotillions, but Northrup makes it clear that his music is lively and included patted percussion from the audience, perhaps very different than how it sounded when he played for a white audience. And although he didn't expand on it much, it is interesting to think that whatever tune Northup might have been playing—including something like the "Virginia Reel"—would have the accompaniment of lyrics and rhythm from the Black attendees.

"Roaring River," Northrup wrote, was a "refrain of the Red River Plantation" and would have been one of the tunes he played for dances and other occasions. The tune is in 2/4 time and G major, and it works well as a fast-tempo, driving fiddle tune.[9] The lyrics, although in dialect and with a racial slur, speak to aspirations of freedom and the reality of oppression.

Northrup was rescued from enslavement in 1853, remarkably, three years after the Fugitive Slave Law passed, when it was even easier for free people to be captured and enslaved.[10] He wrote his memoir as an antislavery text aimed at white audiences and dedicated his book to Harriet Beecher Stowe, the author of *Uncle Tom's Cabin* and a petitioner against the Fugitive Slave Law. His book not only gave a true, firsthand account of the brutality of slavery but showed that even a free Black man might be subject to slavery as long as it was still legal in the United States. And slavery would remain legal for another twelve years after Northrup found his way home.

ROARING RIVER

TRANSCRIPTION

ROARING RIVER

cGCEG (As played by Rhiannon Giddens)
gDGBD (Alternate modern tuning)*

TABLATURE

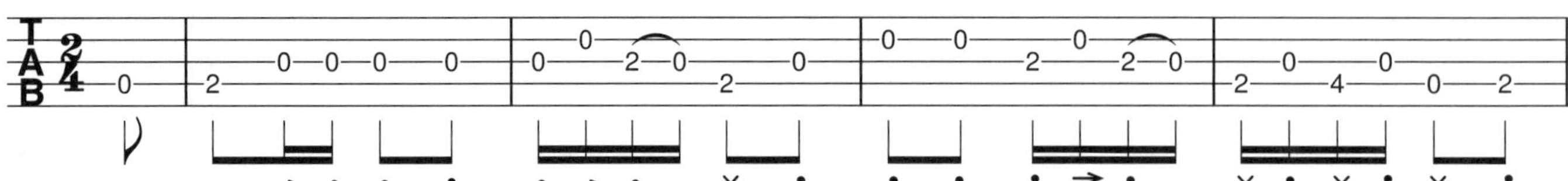

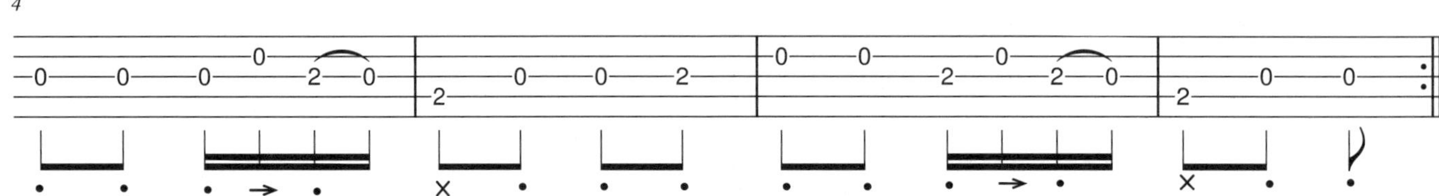

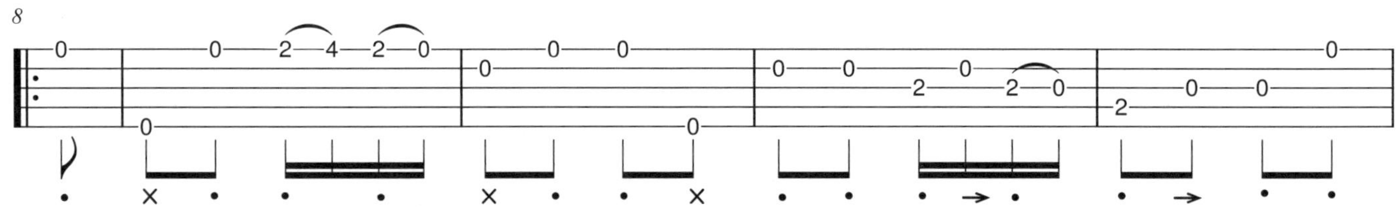

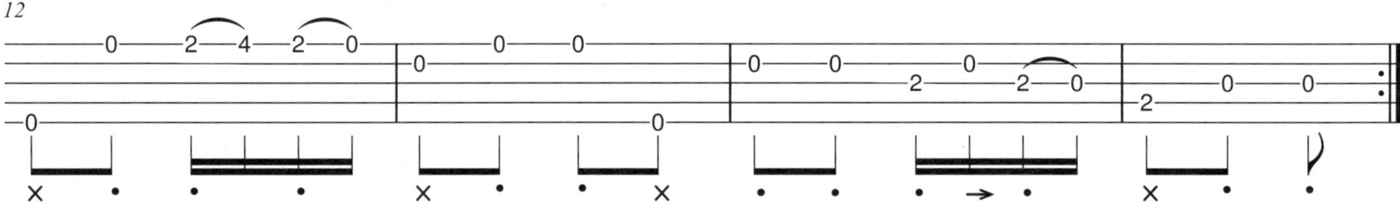

CHAPTER

Tárawan sa de

SURINAME, 1855

"THE BANJA and soesa are as much poetry as song, as much song as dance," Hendrik Charles Focke wrote in the mid-1850s, and he took the time to explain this tradition of Surinamese music and dance in detail.[1] Just as fiddler Solomon Northup's accounts (Piece 9) of his capture and enslavement provide an invaluable view of Black music in the preabolition United States of the 1850s, Focke's proto-ethnomusicology of the Banja, *Soesa*, and music in preabolition Suriname is remarkable. He offered descriptions and musical transcriptions that were based on his experience as a free Afro-Surinamese man proud of his culture. He explained instrumentation, the process by which songs are formed and transmitted, and even included the rhythmic lines that would have accompanied this music. "Tárawan sa de" is one of ten Banja songs he transcribed.

The Banja (also spelled *Banya*) is not a contra dance or set dance but, in the way Focke describes it, more similar to the "jigs" some people describe African Americans dancing. He writes that one man and one woman dance, with a third person joining in on occasion to "provide approval or acclaim" to the dancers. In writing about the Banja, Focke doesn't explore how the dance is also part of the Winti religion, and different versions of the Banja can have different functions, including communication with ancestors.[2] Danced together, these Banjas would create a *Banyaprei* that could last for days.

In the version of the Banja that Focke writes about in the 1850s, the only instruments used are drums. However, the banjo was once a part of the Banja orchestra and may, in fact, have gotten its name from the dance. In his dictionary of 1855 translating Sranan, the creole language spoken in Suriname, to Dutch, Focke writes that the instrument Banja (which soldier John Gabriel Stedman, Piece 3, spelled *bania*) accompanied these dances but wasn't a part of the dance music any longer.[3]

The leader of the song is the *troki-man*, a woman who sings a line that the chorus then repeats. Although others, including Stedman, found this call-and-response song improvisational or impromptu, Focke turns that idea on its head: "The words sung, however insignificant, are rarely ever improvised on the spot," he writes. Instead, the *troki-man* comes up with the lyrics on her own, and then the lyrics are approved by musicians and dancers before being incorporated into the performance.

Focke does admit that this music can seem monotonous, since "only a few words that mean nothing are enough for a song." Here, he may be showing how, as much as he appreciates the Banja, he's not really part of the culture that has created it. He was a free man of color and enslaved people danced the Banja, and so he may not have fully understood the words and their meaning. The lyrics to "Tárawan sa de" reference the *opeté*, or hoatzin, a large tropical bird, and Focke speculates that it may "also be a nickname" that one person has given to another. "There are others, shouts the hoatzin. A man is a man! What do I care?" the song goes. Focke thinks this is "a complaint for disappointed love," with the female singer taking solace in the fact that there are more men in the world. But there could be different meanings Focke didn't pick up on either.

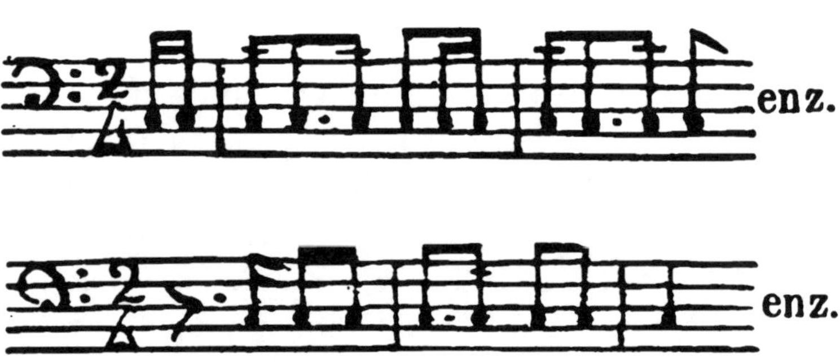

Two rhythmic patterns for the Banja songs, according to H. C. Focke in *West-Indië*. The figure on the left includes a sixteenth note followed by a dotted eighth note, which is present in American jigs and West African dance music.

"Tárawan sa de" in *West-Indië*. One of the Banja songs that H. C. Focke transcribed from music he heard in Suriname before emancipation.

"Tárawan sa de" is in 2/4 time and G minor. The triples throughout the piece provide a three-against-two syncopation.[4] The minor key gives a somber feeling that the editors of *Slave Songs of the United States* felt they heard in music from the South Carolina Sea Islands less than ten years later. Although the Banja music was "unique to Black creoles" in Suriname, Focke thought it had similarities to the "Bamboula of the French colonies and the Banjo of the southern states of North America"—Focke understanding "banjo" to be a style of music and dance.[5] The opening of "Tárawan sa de," does have similarities to "A Poor Wayfaring Stranger," and it is tempting to make a comparison or figure out how they might be related, but when the two melodies are actually compared, they have different rhythms and keys.[6]

Focke transcribed ten Banja songs, two *Soesa* songs, two street songs, and one song from the Ndyuka or Aukan Maroons, perhaps knowing that with abolition on the horizon in Suriname, Afro-Surinamese culture would soon change forever.

TÁRAWAN SA DE

TRANSCRIPTION

cFCFG (As played by Rhiannon Giddens)
gCGCD (Alternate modern tuning)*

TABLATURE

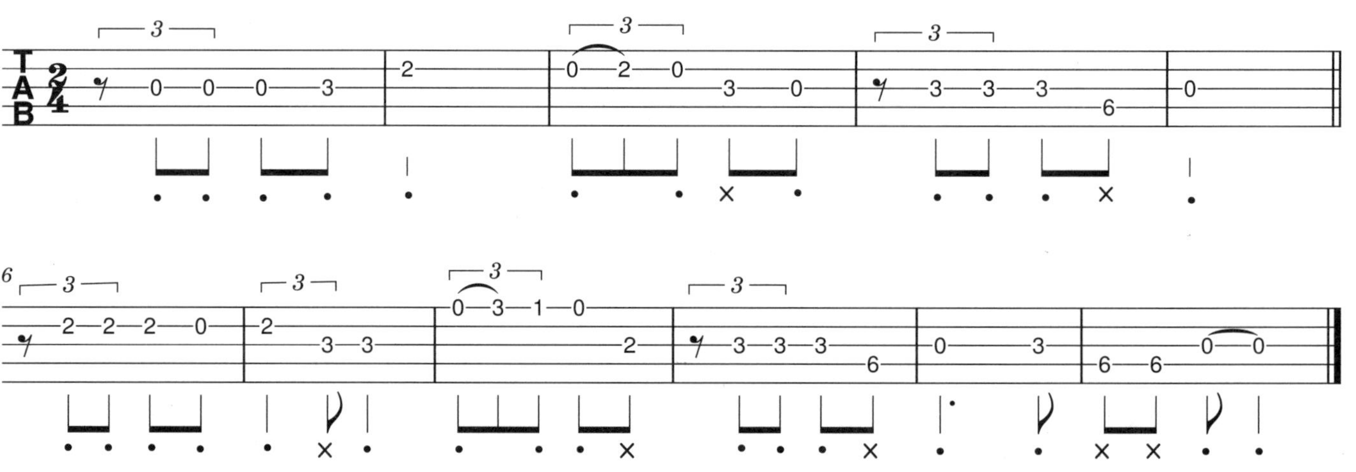

CHAPTER

Throw the Banjo Out of Tune

ELMIRA, NEW YORK, 1850–1851

So Come Along

SOUTHERN UNITED STATES

IN THE early 1850s, a light-skinned Black man would set up somewhere in the town of Elmira, New York, his banjo in hand. He traveled to neighboring villages but probably lived in the town of 8,000 people, since almost all of the Black residents of Chemung County did. A thirteen-year-old white boy named Frank Converse was transfixed by the man, who would be "playing and singing and passing his hat for collections." Converse remembered that when the man had a real crowd, he would play "his piece de resistance." Then, the banjo player would tell the audience gathered that "such a trifling circumstance as the banjo being out of tune caused him no inconvenience"—he was that good. Converse noticed the man throw the banjo out of tune "with a seemingly careless fumbling of the pegs," and although Converse didn't play banjo yet, he was a musician and noticed that the banjo player's "careless fumbling" was anything but that.

Converse went on to become one of the most prominent banjo players of his day, and he remembered the tune so well that he was able to transcribe it fifty years later.[1] We've chosen to call this song "Throw the Banjo Out of Tune," since Converse didn't remember the title or the player. Converse also remembered a second song from the Southern United States we're calling "So Come Along." As ubiquitous as the banjo might have been, these are the only two songs in this collection (and that we know of) explicitly transcribed from Black banjo playing.

In Elmira during those years, most Black male residents had been born in New York, but some came from slave states including

Virginia, Maryland, and North Carolina. Some men didn't provide a birthplace in the 1850 Census—either because they did not know it or because they did not want to reveal where they had come from for fear of the Fugitive Slave Law of 1850 and being kidnapped back into slavery. None of the men had their occupation listed as musician in that census, but there were masons, laborers, barbers, tanners, and boatmen who could have been the banjo player.

Hearing that banjo player changed Frank Converse's life. Although his father did not approve, within a year of hearing the Black man play, Converse got a banjo, and shortly thereafter he learned from Blackface Minstrel Picayune Butler and was inspired by George S. Buckley's Minstrel show. Although Converse couldn't remember the Black player's name, he remembered that the player "was limited to the thumb and first finger,—pulling or 'picking' the strings both." Today, we might call this two-finger up-picking. This style was in contrast to Buckley, who "pulled the strings à la guitar," and Butler, who played "Banjo" or "Stroke" style, what we call clawhammer or downstroke playing today. Two-finger up-picking style also appears decades later in the repertoire of white banjo players, including Uncle Dave Macon, Virgil Anderson, and Roscoe Holcomb, but not in the repertoire of white Blackface Minstrels, suggesting a tradition shared between white and Black players not mediated by Minstrelsy.[2] The tab for "Throw the Banjo Out of Tune" is still written for stroke-style

In his reminiscences in the music publication the *Cadenza*, Frank Converse transcribed two pieces that he heard Black banjoists playing in the mid-nineteenth century.

technique, but we encourage players to try this piece with two-finger up-picking as well.

In describing the playing style of Black banjoists, Converse adds that the "fingering was unique,—requiring only the first finger of the left hand for stopping on the strings—on the first string at the first fret and the second string at the second fret," yet neither of the notations that he has made follow this fingering. On "Throw the Banjo Out of Tune," you have to play on the third string and you have to play up the neck out of the first position. In "So Come Along," you play the third string open and at the second fret. However, you can play both tunes without using more than your first finger.

Converse noticed that the player in Elmira was not careless about this tuning even though he pretended to "throw the banjo out of tune." He was "merely pitching the second string a semitone higher." Raising the pitch of the second string a semitone from the standard tuning of the 1850s and 1860s, would make the banjo tuned eAEAB or cFCFG, which is the same relative pitches as double-C banjo tuning (gCGCD), the most common banjo tuning for songs in C (and D when capoed to the second fret).

Banjoist Lowell Schreyer notes that the piece has "the syncopation characteristic of the later cakewalk," which is the sixteenth-eighth-sixteenth pattern that became a central part of late-nineteenth-century ragtime music.[3] But again, Converse may have found a challenge in transcribing the music. For example, the final E note of measure three, the two A notes in the first half of measure four, and the final E note of measure five are written as thirty-second notes, possibly implying a dotted rhythm. Without the presence of a dot in any of these figures, this is more likely a stylistic direction. Below, the notes are written as sixteenth notes in order to keep rhythmically consistent with the rest of the piece.

Converse doesn't give a name to the second piece either, so we've chosen the chorus "So Come Along." What is unusual in the transcription for "So Come Along" is the vocal melody on the top line and the banjo melody on the second line. Converse wrote that on "Southern plantations," a banjo player "would improvize [*sic*] his song as he went along," not unlike the extemporaneous singing soldier John Gabriel Stedman described in Suriname (Piece 3).

Converse doesn't reveal more about the origins of "So Come Along" and simply said it "seemed quite common."[4] However, the song doesn't appear to have been adopted by the Blackface Minstrels and is not in the compilation *Slave Songs of the United States* (Piece 12). If one of the editors of *Slave Songs* had heard the lyrics "My old massa, he like chicken / My ole missus, she like sugar," they may have thought it related to Minstrelsy and therefore chose not to include it in their collection. Rather than being influenced by Minstrels, however, these lyrics could have been a criticism of the white oppressors. In their analysis of Surinamese song, Melville and Frances Herskovits assert that social criticism in song is a West African practice, and anthropologist Aminata Cairo writes that Banja songs and dances had coded criticism, often of white oppressors.[5] Perhaps the white people liking chicken and sugar provided a critique of their indulgence at a time when enslaved people were regularly and intentionally not given enough food.

THROW THE BANJO OUT OF TUNE

TRANSCRIPTION

cFCFG (As played by Rhiannon Giddens)
gCGCD (Alternate modern tuning)
eAEAB (To play with transcription)

TABLATURE

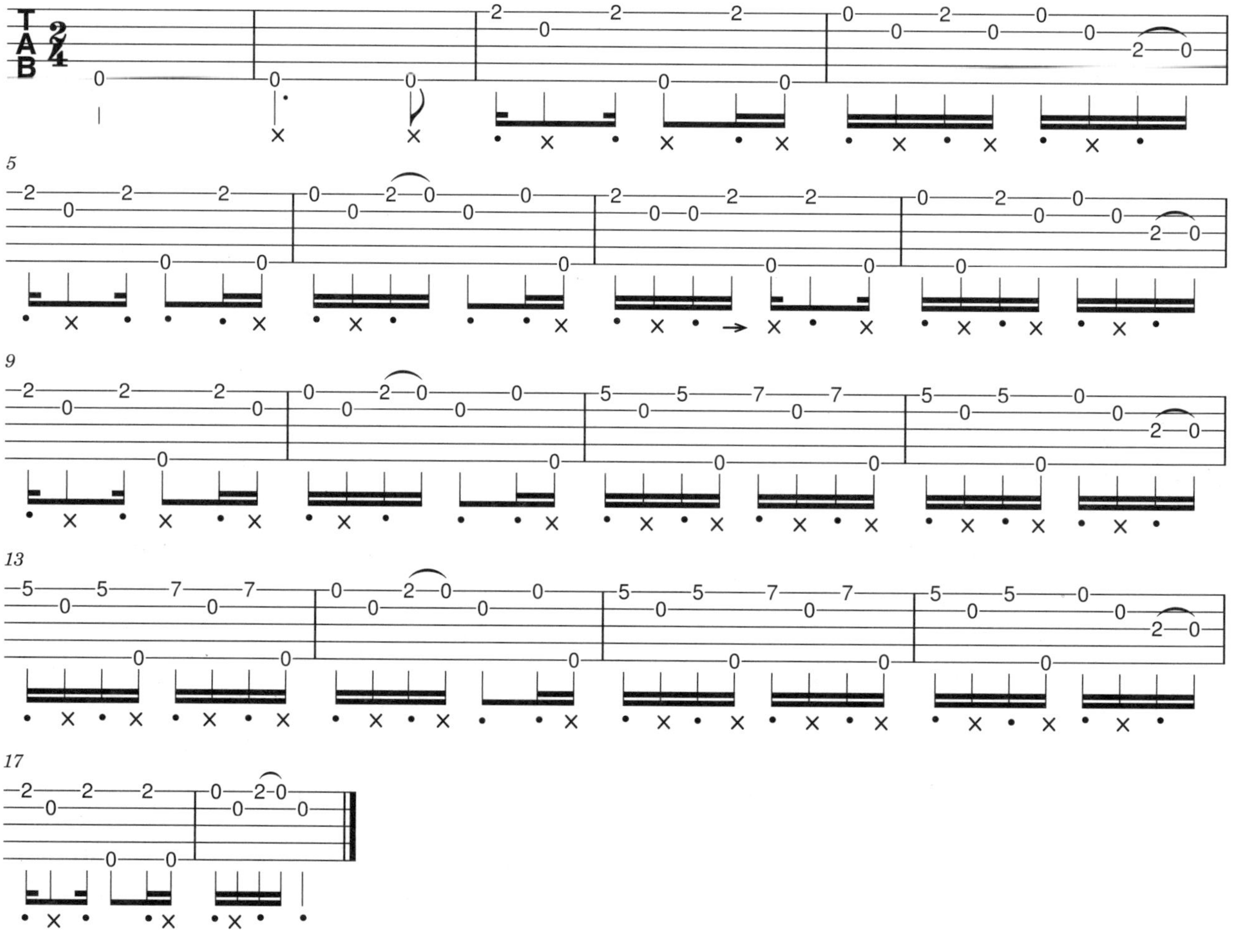

SO COME ALONG

TRANSCRIPTION

cFCEG (As played by Rhiannon Giddens)
gCGBD (Alternate modern tuning)
eAEG♯B (To play with transcription)

TABLATURE

A group of African American women holding babies outside their living quarters on the Sea Islands of South Carolina, possibly on Thomas J. Fripp's plantation on St. Helena Island, between 1863 and June 1866. Hubbard and Mix, photographer, Library of Congress, Washington, DC.

CHAPTER

Poor Rosy

SOUTH CAROLINA, 1862

Round the Corn, Sally!

VIRGINIA, 1860S

Caroline

LOUISIANA, 1850S

PUBLISHED just two years after the end of the Civil War, *Slave Songs of the United States* brought together 136 songs from the Black American tradition across the United States.[1] The editors, William Francis Allen, Charles W. Ware, and Lucy McKim Garrison, felt that although the musical ability of Black Americans had "been recognized for so many years," it was disappointing that more had not been done "to collect and preserve their melodies." Just as William Dickson wanted to prove the "humanity" of enslaved people by writing about music in Barbados, so Allen, Ware, and McKim Garrison wanted to use the music they collected to advocate for Black equality. All three were abolitionists, and since the Civil War was over, they felt that they could use their book to highlight overlooked musical culture and what they called Black genius. We've chosen to include three songs from the collection—"Poor Rosy," "Round the Corn, Sally!" and "Caroline"—to show continuity and adaptation of Black music across centuries and continents.

The editors of *Slave Songs of the United States* admitted to being "fully aware of the incompleteness of this collection" for many reasons. They collected songs and solicited pieces from friends and other abolitionists they knew. In some instances, they received words but not melodies. In others, they could find "strains of familiar tunes," which they deemed okay to include, whereas some songs that could be found in Methodist hymnals they chose to exclude.[2] They also noted that "very few [of the songs] are of an intrinsically barbaric character," by which they meant "purely African in origin."[3] Abolitionists were not all above stereotypes and racism, and the editors felt that even though most of the songs they collected had "a distinct tinge of their native Africa," the music had become more "civilized" through contact with European-derived music.[4] The secular tunes in the collection include work songs, but they couldn't find what they call "fiddle-songs," "devil-songs," "corn-songs," and "jig-tunes." The editors don't explain in detail what the characteristics of these songs are, but "Round the Corn, Sally!" (Piece 12b), "Many Thousand Go," and "Shock Along, John" are secular songs.[5] They also write that they primarily found tunes in South Carolina, where they were working for the freedmen's relief efforts, and they found it hard "to persuade them [the freedpeople] to sing their old songs, even as a curiosity, [as] such is the sense of dignity that has come with freedom."[6] The editors also avoided tunes they knew to be associated with Minstrelsy, even if Black folks were singing them, because they couldn't parse what was part of a vernacular tradition and what was just popular music. The editors imagined a future second volume when they could find more secular songs, but unfortunately that never came to be.

"Poor Rosy"

Lucy McKim couldn't decide if she wanted to laugh or cry as she toured the South Carolina Sea Islands in the summer of 1862 with her father, James Miller McKim. He helped found the Philadelphia Port Royal Relief Association to provide education, clothing, housing, and trade skills to newly freed people in Union-occupied South Carolina.

McKim (she hadn't yet married Wendell Garrison) saw both joy and despair there. On the one hand, a Black cook named Susanna felt "too much happiness" and sang all day long. On the other, McKim could still see the "horrible cruelty" Susanna and the other formerly enslaved people faced.[7] The songs McKim heard seemed to reflect that dichotomy, too, and one woman told Lucy McKim that you couldn't sing "Poor Rosy" without "a full heart and a troubled sperrit!" McKim found "Poor Rosy" so compelling, she transcribed it.

McKim heard both religious and work songs during her brief stay in South Carolina. She thought that the songs she took down could convey something more about the lives of Black people than the abolitionists had yet accomplished. "The wild, sad strains tell, as the sufferers themselves never could, of crushed hopes, keen sorrow, and a dull daily misery which covered them as hopelessly as the fog from the rice swamps," McKim wrote in a letter to John Sullivan Dwight, which he published in his magazine *Dwight's Journal of Music* later that year.

Although she was too demure to say it directly in her letter, McKim's message was political. As the Civil War extended into its second year, some Northern abolitionists wanted to prove that freed people could become equal citizens in the United States

3

POOR ROSY, POOR GAL.

No 1.

Arranged by Miss LUCY McKIM.

Entered according to act of Congress A.D. 1862 by L. McKim in the Clerk's office of the District Court of the Eastern Dist: Court of Pa.

The first page of Lucy McKim's sheet music for "Poor Rosy, Poor Gal" after her return from South Carolina. Garrison Family Papers, Sophia Smith Collection of Women's History, Smith College, Northampton, MA.

and did not need to be sent to places including Haiti, Panama, or Liberia in what the abolitionists called "colonization schemes." When Lucy wrote to Dwight in November 1862, she was thrilled by news of the impending Emancipation Proclamation, which was to take effect on New Year's Day 1863.[8] Even if the melodies of the songs she heard seemed sad, "the words breathe a trusting faith in rest in the future" of freedom.[9]

"Poor Rosy" was one of the work songs McKim and Charles Ware heard on St. Helena Island. While still in South Carolina, McKim wrote that she was "keeping a diary" and had "copied a number" of the songs she heard.[10] However, neither her handwritten notes nor her diary survive in any Garrison family archives. Ware and McKim both wrote the song in E minor, although McKim has it in 4/4 time and Ware writes in 2/4. McKim's version repeats the line "Poor Rosy, poor gal," with slight variations on the melody, while Ware's has more lyrics and a different melody at times.

"As the same songs are sung at every sort of work, of course the tempo is not always alike," Lucy informed Dwight. When men sung "Poor Rosy" while rowing, it was andante; when a girl and boy sang it turning the wheel of the hominy mill, it had to "fly"; and after work, a woman might sing it "slowly and mournfully."[11]

"There is much more in this new and curious music," Lucy writes, "of which it is a temptation to write, but I must remember that it can speak for itself better than any one for it."[12]

Lucy's note in *Dwight's Journal of Music* and publication of "Poor Rosy" and "Roll Jordan Roll" sparked an interest that led to more collection, and ultimately the publication of *Slave Songs of the United States*.[13]

"Round the Corn, Sally!"

A man jumps onto a huge pile of unshucked corn. He's been chosen as captain and begins to sing a song that will let everyone know that the corn shucking is about to begin.[14] That song could have been "Round the Corn, Sally!" People might come from neighboring plantations; even though they are enslaved, they've been allowed to have this party, not unlike the Calindas and *Banya* plays in the Caribbean. It was a big honor to be elected captain of the corn shucking, to come up with work songs that would set the pace.[15] If someone found a red ear, they might be made queen or king of the festivities.[16] When the shucking was over, there would be more dancing and feasting.

"Round the Corn, Sally!" is a work song, like "Poor Rosy." In *Slave Songs of the United States*, William Francis Allen writes that the tune is from Virginia, and he named it as one of the "barbaric" songs they found.[17] He doesn't reveal what he really means by that, and there are any number of reasons he might think that, including the lyrics, rhythm, or melody. "'Iggle' is of course 'eagle,'" Allen writes, "for the rest of the enigmatical words and expressions in this corn-song, we must leave readers to guess at the interpretation."[18] He doesn't seem to understand the word "count-aquils" or what "ginny bank the weaver" means. The song is notated in 2/4 but clearly syncopated, for example, with a sixteenth-eighth-sixteenth pattern in the second part of the first measure and a sixteenth-eighth pattern in the second part of the second measure. This rhythmic pattern is seen in American jigs and West African dance music that predate *Slave Songs* and became a basic feature of ragtime rhythms of the twentieth century, according to historian Roland Nadeau.[19]

There is a corn shucking in *The Valley of Shenandoah*, by George Tucker, a novel published in 1824 about "early nineteenth century Virginia life" based on Tucker's own experiences.[20] Tucker was born in the British colony of Bermuda, moved to Virginia in 1795 at the age of twenty, and eventually owned land and enslaved people. Writing from a different experience than that of the Bolling family in Virginia who notated "Congo" (Piece 7), Tucker felt "so entirely separated are the two classes of black and white" that there were many white folks who've never heard a corn song. "Some one, who feels himself qualified for the office, strikes up, and singly gives a few rude stanzas, sometimes in rhyme, and sometimes in short expressive sentences, while the rest unite in chorus, and this he continues, until some other improvisatore relieves him," one of Tucker's characters explains in the novel.[21]

Cornhusking to the music of the fiddle in *Harper's Weekly*, April 13, 1861.

The early Blackface performers thought that corn-shucking music was authentic, and they wanted to emulate it on stage. And interestingly, Tucker's novel was published right before what is considered one of the first published Blackface sheet music compositions, "Coal Black Rose," in 1828.[22] By 1843, the Virginia Minstrels claimed they would perform "songs, refrains, and ditties as sung by the southern slaves at all their merry meetings such as the gathering in the cotton and sugar crops, corn shuckings, slave weddings, and junketings."[23] Thomas Briggs includes his version of a "Corn Shucking Jig" in his banjo instruction book from 1855 (which, although in 2/4 time, uses sets of triplets that can make it feel like 12/8 time).[24] Christy's Minstrels sung a tune called "O Come to De Husking," composed by Frank Spencer, before 1848. As with almost every tune that appears in the Blackface Minstrel repertoire, we can't be sure of the song's origins, but because music and dance were integral to corn shuckings, perhaps they chose these titles to appear authentic, or they could have based their songs on actual vernacular Black tradition.

As the editors of *Slave Songs of the United States* pointed out, without a better record of Black music, it was hard to discern the origins and transformations of songs. A decade and a half into the pop-culture phenomenon that was Blackface Minstrelsy, James Hungerford's novel *The Old Plantation and What I Gathered There in an Autumn Month* (1859) included music and lyrics to "Round the Corn, Sally!," which is a different tune with different lyrics and changes from 4/4 time to 6/8 time partway through the song.[25] This could have been something Hungerford made up, something he heard on the Minstrel stage, or simply a regional variation of the tune. There is also a sea shanty with the title "Round the Corner, Sally!," and by the time Cecil Sharp transcribed it in 1914, the key, time signature, and lyrics were all different from the "Round the Corn, Sally!" in *Slave Songs* and Hungerford's novel.[26] This doesn't mean that they couldn't have a similar origin point. A sea shanty is just a work song—meant to control the cadence of pulling ropes or rowing oars—and *shanty* may come from the French word *chanter* (to sing).[27]

"Caroline"

People enslaved on the Good Hope plantation in St. Charles Parish sang the seven Louisiana pieces that appear in *Slave Songs of the United States*, including "Caroline."[28] The editors say only that "a lady" heard them sung there and offer no information about the people who sang the songs. Good Hope would have resembled a plantation in Suriname more so than one in Maryland, with river access at the front of the property and sugarcane fields at the back, and the houses where enslaved people lived—and likely made music—in between.[29]

They do write that "Caroline" is a *coonjai*, "a simple dance, a sort of minuet," a dance different from the Calinda. The historic record doesn't have good descriptions of the *coonjai* (also spelled *counjaille*) before the publication of *Slave Songs of the United States*. However, the dance might be related to or a derivation of Congo dances (see "Congo," Piece 7).[30] Both in New Orleans and outside the city, white observers made note of Congo dances to the music of the banjo before the Civil War.[31] Seventy-two years after the publication of *Slave Songs* and after George Washington Cable made the dances of Congo Square famous with his reminiscences in the 1880s, Jeanne Arguedas recorded what she called Creole songs from New Orleans in 1939 as part of the Works Progress Administration's Federal Writers' Project. Arguedas designated herself as a Creole, but census takers only marked her and her family as white going back generations.[32] She recorded both "Coundja ape vini," which she designates as a Vodou chant, and "Un, deux, trois, Caroline."[33] In 1937, Alan Lomax recorded a man he only calls Audebert at the Lafont Catholic Old Folks' Home singing "Danse la Counjaille."[34]

In 1860s Louisiana, the music for "Caroline" was "furnished by an orchestra of singers," including a leader who improvises a line and a chorus that responds. In addition to singers, someone would provide rhythm on "the barrelhead-drum, the jaw-bone and key, or some other rude instrument."

"Caroline" is in G major and 4/4 time, and although the editors of slave songs characterize it as "a sort of minuet," minuets are typically in triple time. Perhaps the original observer thought of it this way because a man and woman danced together, rather than it being a circle dance or one with couples who mixed. Even though G major and 4/4 time may seem basic, the vocal and melodic phrases begin just before the measure and end with a rest, giving the whole piece a forward momentum.

POOR ROSY

TRANSCRIPTION

ROUND THE CORN, SALLY!

TRANSCRIPTION

cFCEG (As played by Rhiannon Giddens)
gCGBD (Alternate modern tuning)
fB♭FAC (To play with transcription)

TABLATURE

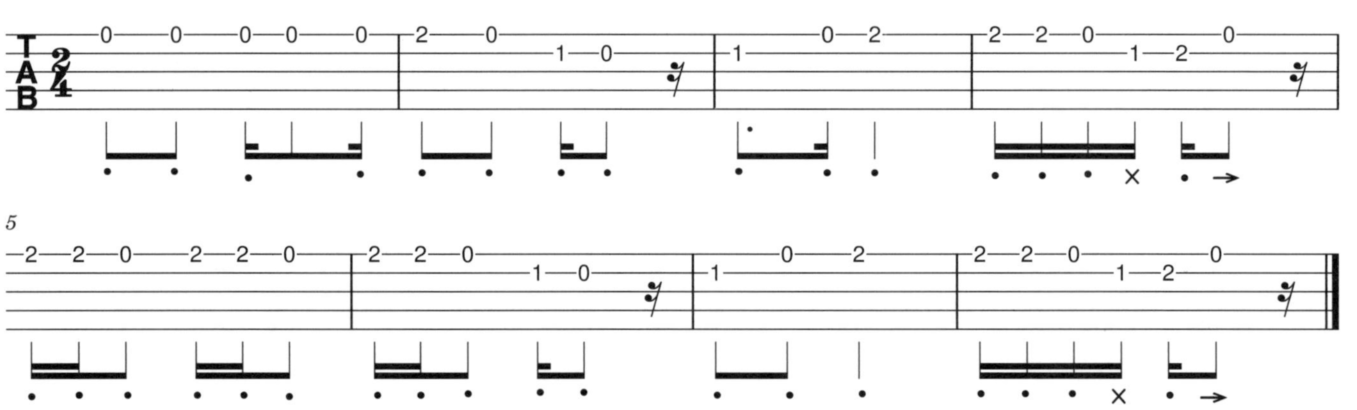

CAROLINE

TRANSCRIPTION

cFCEG (As played by Rhiannon Giddens)
gCGBD (Alternate modern tuning)
dGDF♯A (To play with transcription)

TABLATURE

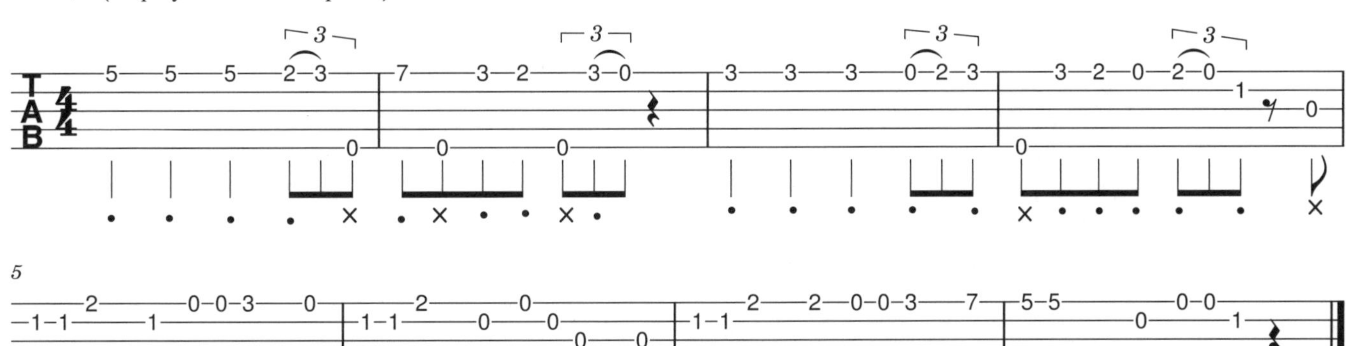

Alternate Final Measure

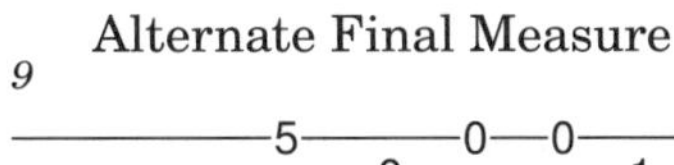

The tune “Genuine Negro Jig” as it appears in Dan Emmett’s manuscript. Courtesy of Ohio History Connection, Columbus.

CHAPTER

Snowden's Jig

OHIO, 1850S

THE WHOLE family would gather on the second-story gable of their house, a feature that made their home a stage. Folks from around Mount Vernon, Ohio, knew the free Black musicians of the Snowden family, and people would cross the street from Smith's Tavern to hear them play.[1] Ellen Snowden might begin a song while her son Ben and daughters Sophia and Annie harmonized on violin melody lines, with rhythm and accompaniment coming from little brother Lew on the banjo or tambourine and little sister Elcy dancing.[2] Earlier in the 1850s, some members of the family band had traveled with their father, Thomas Snowden, to perform, but he had died in July 1856.[3] A handbill advertised the family as "self-taught," with performances on "violin, triangle, and dulcimer, with castinet [*sic*] accompaniments."[4] They might have played Stephen Foster's composition for the Minstrel stage "My Old Kentucky Home" or a song they wrote themselves, including a jig that now goes by the name "Snowden's Jig."[5]

By the time the Snowdens performed at their home, Blackface Minstrelsy was hugely popular. Former Mount Vernon resident Daniel Decatur Emmett had made his name as a Blackface musician, and folks around the area knew that he was interested in the music of the Snowden family. For his performance persona, it behooved Emmett to produce music that seemed authentically Black, and so he could have taken a tune or two from the Snowden family. He might have heard a tune and transcribed it or simply asked the Snowdens to write him a song. Locals said it was in fact the Snowdens who wrote "Dixie," which would become Emmett's most famous tune.[6]

Emmett had less well known tunes that may have come from the Snowden family. In his handwritten manuscript, Emmett transcribed a tune he called "Genuine Negro Jig," which the Carolina Chocolate Drops played and titled "Snowden's Jig" in honor of the Snowdens.[7]

In their exploration of the relationship between the Snowdens and Dan Emmett,

Howard Sacks and Judith Sacks write that Emmett taking music from or being inspired by the Snowdens may have been emblematic of "significant black-white musical exchange . . . on the frontier . . . [which] was subsequently distorted for mass consumption on the urban minstrel stage."[8] This exchange makes sense: musicologist Christopher J. Smith writes that canals, rivers, and other waterways were points of mixture between Black, white American, and European immigrant populations and provided a place for musical creolization. That Black-white musical exchange also happened across the Americas before the 1810s, as "Black Dance" (Piece 6) and "Congo" (Piece 7) exemplify.

The transformation of "Genuine Negro Jig" to "Snowden's Jig" is also about more than just a name change. This is a piece that was tucked away in a handwritten manuscript in an archive and published in an obscure book until it landed in the hands of the Carolina Chocolate Drops. But they didn't just play it exactly as written, since most traditional-folk-vernacular music can't be captured by notes on a page. Rhiannon's musical apprenticeship with Joe Thompson of Mebane, North Carolina, influenced her playing and understanding of the written notes on Emmett's pages and how a player of the Black string band tradition in the United States would have approached that music. For the banjo tab, Rhiannon has taken what Emmett wrote out over two octaves and arranged it into a single octave. This makes the tune more accessible to contemporary banjo players. We're including Rhiannon's transformed and adapted version of "Snowden's Jig" to show how we might all use our musical influences and backgrounds to make the historic notes on the pages of this book come alive again. ௸

SNOWDEN'S JIG

TRANSCRIPTION

SNOWDEN'S JIG

TABLATURE

cFCEG (As played by Rhiannon Giddens)*
gCGBD (Alternate modern tuning)

ACKNOWLEDGMENTS

THANK YOU TO Cate Hodorowicz and the team at UNC Press for making an idea a book. To the behind-the-scenes people: Megan Frestedt, Melantha Hodge, and Laura Nolan. To David Elsenbroich and Greg Adams for meticulous help with the banjo tabs.

We stand on the shoulders of other researchers: Specific thanks go to Devin Thomas Leigh for his research and providing images of the "Jamaican Airs," to Mary Caton Lingold for her work on Mr. Baptiste, to Fredrik Thomasson for his work on Christopher Carlander and Saint-Barthélemy's music, to Eric Johnson-DeBaufre for the image of Elizabeth Van Rensselaer's music book and assistance with the manuscript research, and to Matthew Turi for finding the "Congo" reference at UNC Library.

To our families for help and support: Pete Ross and Clifford Gaddy for reading, research, providing feedback and being honest; Aoife and Caoimhin for their patience.

NOTES

UNDERSTANDING THIS MUSIC

1. Allen, Ware, and McKim Garrison, *Slave Songs of the United States*, i.
2. While *white* can be a contentious term, the people of European descent who recorded these tunes would have considered themselves definitely non-Black and likely white.
3. See, for example, Thornton, "Religious and Ceremonial Life"; and Dewulf, *Pinkster King and the King of the Kongo*.
4. Jefferson, *Notes on the State of Virginia*, 257; Edwards, *History*, ii, 84.
5. In this book, we capitalize the terms *Blackface*, *Minstrel*, and *Minstrelsy* to distinguish the popular cultural movement that is Blackface Minstrelsy from blackface in general, which would be anyone imitating a Black person with face paint, and from the generic definition of *minstrelsy*, which has been used going back to the fourteenth century to define medieval musicians. We use the words *Minstrelsy* or *Minstrel* as shorthand for *Blackface Minstrel* or *Blackface Minstrelsy*.
6. Chernoff, "Rhythmic Medium in African Music," 1096.
7. Sloane, *Voyage to the Islands*, 1.
8. Pinckard, *Notes on the West Indies*, 263–69.
9. Chernoff, "Rhythmic Medium in African Music," 1097.
10. Chernoff, "Rhythmic Medium in African Music," 1098.
11. Jamison, *Hoedowns, Reels, and Frolics*, 68.
12. Raboteau, *Slave Religion*, 15.
13. Douglass, *Narrative*, 74–75.
14. Desch-Obi, "Combat and the Crossing of the *Kalunga*," 358; Njoku, "Idioms of Religion, Music, Dance, and African Art Forms," 174; Epstein, *Sinful Tunes*, 24.
15. Floyd, "Black Music in the Cirum-Caribbean," 1.
16. See Epstein's *Sinful Tunes*; Dubois's *Banjo*; and Gaddy's *Well of Souls*.
17. Gaddy, "Banjo before Stringbands."
18. Pinckard, *Notes on the West Indies*, 315, 352.
19. Gaddy, "Banjo before Stringbands."
20. Chernoff, "Rhythmic Medium in African Music," 1096.
21. Chernoff writes, "It would be difficult to find an African musical tradition that did not contain this rhythm, and, similarly, the rhythm frequently supports many pieces in many traditions' repertories." "Rhythmic Medium in African Music," 1096.
22. Agawu, "Structural Analysis or Cultural Analysis?," 9–10.
23. Labat, *Nouveau voyage*, 463–69. Although *calinda* has many different names (see "Calemba" and "The Colymba"), we are standardizing it to *calinda* unless in the quotation of a source.
24. Chernoff, "Rhythmic Medium in African Music," 1096.
25. Stedman, *Stedman's Suriname*, 278.

PLAYING THIS MUSIC

1. On pages 9 and 10 of *Briggs' Banjo Instructor*, Briggs explains how mid-nineteenth-century banjos were tuned and how to do these relative tunings. The book is available online at https://archive.org/details/briggsbanjoinstroobrig. Jim Dalton also explores tunings in his chapter "The Changing Intonational Practice of Mid-Nineteenth-Century Banjo" in *Banjo Roots and Branches*.

CHAPTER 1

1. Sloane, *Voyage to the Islands*, 1.
2. Taylor, *Jamaica in 1687*, 269; Beckford, *Descriptive Account of the Island of Jamaica*, 120–21; Lingold, *African Musicians in the Atlantic World*, chap. 4.
3. Cogdell Djedje, "Song Type," 166.
4. Heywood and Thornton, *Central Africans, Atlantic Creoles*, 81–82.
5. For more on the names, see Rath, "African Music in Seventeenth-Century Jamaica," 709–10.
6. Rath, "African Music in Seventeenth-Century Jamaica," 725–26.
7. Schöpf, *Travels in the Confederation*, 262.
8. Bowdich, *Mission from Cape Coast Castle to Ashantee*, 279.
9. Sloane, *Voyage to the Islands*, lii.
10. Sloane, *Voyage to the Islands*, xlviii–xlix.
11. Sloane, *Voyage to the Islands*, 1.
12. Chernoff, "Rhythmic Medium in African Music," 1098.
13. Pinn, *Varieties of African American Religious Experience*, 13.
14. Fernández Olmos and Paravisini-Gebert, *Creole Religions of the Caribbean*, 121; Lichtveld and Voorhoeve, *Creole Drum*, 18.
15. Nathan, *Dan Emmett*, 195.
16. Chernoff, "Rhythmic Medium in African Music," 1097.
17. Chernoff, "Rhythmic Medium in African Music," 1098; Lingold, Dubois, and Garner, *Musical Passage*.
18. Chernoff, "Rhythmic Medium in African Music," 1097. In "Papa," notes do not fall on the downbeat, providing what many people call syncopation, which is associated with African rather than European music. However, Chernoff argues that "notions like syncopation and offbeat accentuation would not seem to make sense" in the polyrhythmic context. Lingold, Dubois, and Garner, "Koromanti (1)," *Musical Passage*. Their website provides a wealth of information and analysis on Baptiste's transcriptions, as well as arrangements of the pieces.

CHAPTER 2

1. Pinckard, *Notes on the West Indies*, 263–69. Although Handler and Frisbie note the presence of fiddles, banjos and fiddles together don't appear as a combination in Barbados.
2. Handler and Frisbie, "Aspects of Slave Life in Barbados," 27–28.
3. There are references to Dickson being in Barbados both for thirteen years, starting in 1772, and for just seven years, from 1772 to 1779.
4. Dickson, *Letters on Slavery*, 93.
5. Dickson, *Mitigation of Slavery*, 346.
6. Dickson, *Letters on Slavery*, iii.
7. Handler and Frisbie, "Aspects of Slave Life in Barbados," 23n–24n.
8. Dickson, *Letters on Slavery*, 74.
9. Handler and Frisbie, "Aspects of Slave Life in Barbados," 23n–24n.
10. See the full catalog record: "An African Song or Chant from Barbados," [late 18th cent], D3549 /13/3/27, Gloucestershire Archives, UK, https://catalogue.gloucestershire.gov.uk/records/D3549/1/3/8/3/2/8.
11. Handler and Frisbie, "Aspects of Slave Life in Barbados," 26. See their essay for an extensive discussion of music and dance in Barbados.
12. Roger P. Gibbs and Julie Courtenay, "Nomination Form International Memory of the World Register: An African Song or Chant from Barbados," July 2016, https://web.archive.org/web/20210513060840/https://en.unesco.org/sites/default/files/barbados_uk_song_eng.pdf.
13. "An African Song or Chant" transcription.
14. Green, "Winti and Christianity," 251–76; Thompson, *Flash of the Spirit*, 109.

CHAPTER 3

1. Stedman, *Stedman's Suriname*, 261. The introduction to this version of Stedman's memoir by Richard and Sally Price extensively explains the differences among Stedman's journals, memoir manuscript, and published book.
2. Gaddy explores Stedman and Joanna's relationship further in *Well of Souls*, chap. 7.

3. Stedman, *Stedman's Suriname*, 268–69.
4. Stedman, *Stedman's Suriname*, 280.
5. Stedman, *Stedman's Suriname*, 159.
6. Stedman, *Stedman's Suriname*, 243.
7. Stedman, *Stedman's Suriname*, 263.

CHAPTER 4

1. Thomas Thistlewood, November 20, 1773, diary, Thistlewood Papers.
2. Browne, "Surviving Slavery," 32.
3. Gaddy, *Well of Souls*, 53.
4. Leigh, "Jamaican Airs," 463. See the online "Jamaican Airs Exhibit" created by Devin Thomas Leigh for the other songs: Early Caribbean Digital Archive, Northeastern University, 2019, https://ecda.northeastern.edu/jamaican-music-exhibit-leigh.
5. Gerstin, "Tangled Roots," 5.
6. Fernández Olmos and Paravisini-Gebert, *Creole Religions*, 132.
7. Edwards, *History*, 84.
8. Luffman, *Brief Account of the Island of Antigua*, 135.
9. Schuler, *Alas, Alas, Kongo*, 83.
10. Leigh, "Author's Notes on Music," transcribed from images © British Library Board, C. E. Long Papers, Add. MS 12405, fols. 335r–341v.

CHAPTER 5

1. The whole collection is available online: "A Selection of Scotch, English, Irish, and Foreign Airs: Adapted to the Fife, Violin or German-Flute," 1782, Glasgow: Printed and sold by James Aird, National Library of Scotland, https://archive.org/details/selectionofscotcooingl.
2. Pendlebury, "Tune Families and Tune Histories," 85. Another version is in Luther Kingsley's Music Book, held at the Mansfield Historical Society in Connecticut.
3. Wells, "Fiddling as an Avenue of Black-White Musical Interchange," 141.
4. *Concise Historical Account*, 213.
5. Cresswell, *Journal*, 52–53.

CHAPTER 6

1. Carlander, *Resejournal*, 54. Carlander calls her "Queen Christina" and says that she has rowed to Saint-Barthélemy from Nevis—if she were white, I think he would name her Ms. or Mrs., and rowing from one Leeward island to another was probably not something a white woman would need to do. (All translations of Carlander's journal and Thomasson's book are by Kristina R. Gaddy.)
2. Keller et al., "Early American Secular Music."
3. Carlander, *Resejournal*, 74.
4. Carlander, *Resejournal*, 53.
5. Thomasson, *Svarta St. Barthelemy*, 19.
6. Carlander, *Resejournal*, 77.
7. Carlander, *Resejournal*, 74–75.
8. Carlander, *Resejournal*, 75.
9. Carlander, *Resejournal*.
10. Carlander, *Resejournal*, 76; Thomasson, *Svarta St. Barthelemy*, 130.
11. Carlander, *Resejournal*, 76.
12. Williams, *Tour through the Island of Jamaica*, 62–64.
13. Gerlach, "Black Arson in Albany," 301–12; Dewulf, "Rediscovering a Hudson Valley Folkloric Tradition," 17.
14. Dewulf explains,

> On July 17, 1804, the Albany Common Council passed a law "to regular the amusements of the Negroes of the City of Albany during the Whitsuntide holidays," which stipulated that "no white persons shall during the Whitsuntide holiday erect or put up any Boothe or Tent within the said City near to or where the Negroes shall erect or put up theirs, nor shall any white persons expose for sale any beer, Cyder, mead, spirituous liquors, or cake, crackers or any other kind of Refreshment at the place or places where the Negroes shall meet to carry on their said amusements."

Pinkster King and the King of the Kongo, 166. For more on Pinkster and Black music and dance, see also Gaddy, *Well of Souls*, chap. 11.

CHAPTER 7

1. Hubard Family Papers, music score book, unknown author, 1790–92, 1810, 1825.
2. Lynda J. Morgan, "Samuel P. Bolling (1819–1900)," *Encyclopedia Virginia*, https://encyclopediavirginia.org/entries/bolling-samuel-p-1819-1900.
3. Robertson, *Pocahontas*, 68–69.
4. Chattleton, "Music and Monticello's Enslaved Community."
5. Flint, *Recollections of the Last Ten Years*, 139–40.
6. Holmes, *Account of the United States*, 322.
7. "The Congo Dance," *Times Picayune* (New Orleans), October 18, 1843.
8. Métraux, *Voodoo in Haiti*, 191.
9. Some scholars have written about this as a "Congé" dance, but *congé* is a dance move rather than the name of a dance itself.
10. Carlander, *Resejournal*, 75.
11. Davis, *Travels*, 148–60. For a more full analysis of the story, see Dubois, *Banjo*.
12. Richard Dobbs Spaight to Joseph Caldwell, July 5, 1797, University of North Carolina Papers, no. 40005. Some have suggested that Stephen Perrin was a refugee from the Haitian Revolution.
13. Saltator, *Treatise on Dance*, 73.
14. Fermin, *Nieuwe algemeene beschryving van de colonie van Suriname*; Pinckard, *Notes*, 353. See and hear Ignatius Sancho's minuet here: "I. Sancho: Minuets, Cotillons & Country Dances (c. 1767) - Minutes 1–3," Sound Heritage, University of Southampton, https://sound-heritage.ac.uk/dance/sancho-minuets-cotillons-country-dances-c1767.
15. See Richard Powers, "Congo Minuet," for the dance steps, original notes from 1802, and contemporary re-creations at https://socialdance.stanford.edu/syllabi/congo_minuet.htm.

CHAPTER 8

1. Geggus, "Haitian Voodoo in the Eighteenth Century," 31; Bercy, *De Saint-Domingue*.
2. Dubois, *Avengers of the New World*, 100–101.
3. Quoted in Thornton, "African Dimensions of the Stono Rebellion," 1102–3.
4. Handler and Bilby, "On the Early Use," 32. For more on the rebellion in Jamaica, see Brown, *Tacky's Revolt*.
5. Prest, "Pale Imitations," 13.
6. Pettinger, "'Eh! Eh! Bomba, Hen! Hen!,'" 83–85.
7. For more exploration of these songs, see Gaddy, *Well of Souls*, 98, 117.
8. Geggus, "Haitian Voodoo," 26–27.
9. Herskovits and Herskovits, *Suriname Folk-Lore*, 96.

CHAPTER 9

1. Northrup, *Twelve Years a Slave*, 217.
2. Northrup, *Twelve Years a Slave*, 79.
3. Northrup, *Twelve Years a Slave*, 181–82.
4. See Winans, "Black Musicians in Eighteenth-Century America."
5. Franklin, "Early Black Spirituality," 8; Leslie, *Low Country Shamanism*, 69.
6. Northrup, 213–20.
7. "The Congo Dance," *Times Picayune*, October 18, 1843.
8. Northrup, *Twelve Years a Slave*, 285.
9. Bascom Lamar Lunsford (from Western North Carolina) and Monte Sano Crowder (from Huntsville, Alabama) played tunes called "Roaring River."
10. The law made it easier for enslavers to find people who had liberated themselves and reenslave them, even if those people lived in states where slavery was illegal. The federal government was also complicit: federal marshals executed the warrants of arrest for fugitives, and the hearings, where the accused fugitives were not allowed to testify on their own behalf, took place in federal court.

CHAPTER 10

1. Focke, "De Surinaamsche negermuzijk," 90–91.
2. Guda, "Banya," 615.
3. Focke, "Banja."
4. A note on the treble clef notation: Measure one of the original transcription seems to be missing an eighth note triplet on beat one. If there

was a triplet connecting the first three eighth notes, the rhythm of measure one would be consistent with the rhythms in measures three, four, six, eight, and nine. The triplet, however, is omitted here in order to accurately reflect the original transcription. Measure eleven is either missing an eighth note triplet on beat one, as in measure one, or the final note G is meant to be an eighth note, not a quarter note, as it appears in the original transcription. Here the triplet is omitted, and the final G note is written as a quarter note in order to accurately reflect the original transcription, even though this creates an irregular number of beats.

5. Focke, "De Surinaamsche negermuzijk," 90–91.
6. "I Am a Pilgrim and a Stranger" was published without music in a hymnary of 1858 and later appears in *Times of Refreshing: A Winnowed Collection of Gospel Hymns and Songs*, by W. T. Dale, in 1896 with the note that it is an "Old Camp-meeting chorus." Visit https://hymnary.org/hymn/CS1858/23; and https://hymnary.org/page/fetch/TRWC1896/23/high.

CHAPTER 11

1. Converse, "Banjo Reminiscences II," 4. All quotations by Converse in this chapter are from this article, available at https://archive.org/details/conversereminiscences/mode/1up.
2. Converse even says, "I cannot say that I learned anything from his execution" of the two-finger style, suggesting that it wasn't helpful to playing Blackface Minstrel tunes. Banjo player Pete Ross adds that "the tune 'Where Did You Come From' [in Phil Rice's 1858 banjo primer] seems most likely to be played in this tuning as well, and the title is associated with Sweeney—one Minstrel most definitively connected to Black vernacular sources. This seems to me to underline the existence of this tuning at the vernacular Black level, where Sweeney learned it, and it became part of a shared tradition." Interview with Kristina R. Gaddy, April 22, 2024.
3. Schreyer, "Banjo in Ragtime," 57.
4. "So Come Along" is in E minor, but it seems as though the C-sharp in the second measure of the banjo part should be a C-natural, since it is on the vocal line. The top system of measure seven in the original transcription is an incomplete measure and seems to be missing the eighth note rest that appears on the "and" of beat two in the top system of measure five. Here the eighth note rest on the "and" of beat two in measure seven has been added in order to make it a complete measure and also to keep the rhythm consistent with measure five.
5. Herskovits and Herskovits, *Suriname Folk-Lore*, 23. Cairo, "Hebi Sani," 242.

CHAPTER 12

1. We encourage everyone to explore the full collection of *Slave Songs of the United States* online at https://archive.org/details/slavesongsofunit ooalle.
2. Allen, Ware, and McKim Garrison, *Slave Songs of the United States*, vi.
3. Allen, Ware, and McKim Garrison, *Slave Songs of the United States*, vii.
4. Allen, Ware, and McKim Garrison, *Slave Songs of the United States*, x.
5. These songs are not religious and mention corn, and they have the call-and-response vocal melodies that seem to characterize the songs the editors imagine.
6. Allen, Ware, and McKim Garrison, *Slave Songs of the United States*, x.
7. "Extracts from Lucy's Letter," June 12, 1863, Garrison Family Papers.
8. Lucy McKim to Ellen Wright, October 1, 1862, Garrison Family Papers.
9. McKim Garrison, "Songs of the Port Royal 'Contrabands,'" 254.
10. Lucy McKim (Garrison) to Ellen Wright (Garrison), June 12, 1863, Garrison Family Papers.
11. McKim Garrison, "Songs of the Port Royal 'Contrabands.'"
12. McKim Garrison, "Songs of the Port Royal 'Contrabands,'" 255.

13. For more on McKim Garrison's work in putting together *Slave Songs of the United States*, see Charters, *Songs of Sorrow*.
14. Quoted in Winslow, "Negro Corn-Shucking," 61.
15. Lowery, *Life on the Old Plantation*, 283.
16. Abrahams, *Singing the Master*, 62.
17. Allen is listed as the transcriber, but he didn't spend time in Virginia, so he likely got it from someone else.
18. Allen, Ware, and McKim Garrison, *Slave Songs*, 68.
19. Nadeau, "Grace and Beauty of Classic Rags," 212.
20. See the introduction to Tucker, *Valley of Shenandoah*, for more on Tucker's biography.
21. Tucker, *Valley of Shenandoah*, 116–17.
22. The date of "Coal Black Rose" sheet music is estimated to be 1828, but the song appears in *Riley's Flute Melodies*, from 1826.
23. Quoted in Nathan, *Dan Emmett*, 120.
24. Briggs, *Briggs' Banjo Instructor*, 19.
25. Hungerford, *Old Plantation*, 190–91.
26. Sharp, *English Folk-Chanteys*, 47. Cecil Sharp was a problematic collector of songs; see Whisnant's *All That Is Native and Fine* for more on Sharp and his collecting.
27. Terry, "Sea Songs and Shanties," 136.
28. Allen, Ware, and McKim, *Slave Songs of the United States*, 113.
29. Today this is the town of Norco and the Good Hope Oil and Gas Field. See "Good Hope Plantation - Image," St. Charles Parish Museum and Historical Association, 2025, https://scphistory.org/gmedia/19th_century_page_069_image_0002-jpg.
30. *Nation*, June 11, 1874, 380–81.
31. Gaddy, *Well of Souls*, 131, 134–36.
32. The full complexity of white, Black, and Creole folklore and folklorists in New Orleans is explored in Gipson, "'Strange, Ventriloquous Voice.'"
33. Halpert, Herbert, and Jeanne W. Arguedas, "Coundja Ape Vini" and "Un, deux, trois, Caroline," June, 1939, AFC 1939/005, American Folklife Collection, Library of Congress, Washington, DC.
34. Lomax, John A. and [Cecile?] Audebert, "Danse la Counjaille," March 1937, AFS 00889 A01, American Folklife Collection, Library of Congress, Washington, DC.

CHAPTER 13

1. Sacks and Sacks, "Way Up North in Dixie," 414.
2. Sacks and Sacks, "Way Up North in Dixie," 413.
3. "Thomas Snowden," *FindAGrave* index, www.findagrave.com/memorial/214565382/thomas-snowden. Lewis "Lew" was born 1848 and Elcy in 1854, so they may have been too young to be part of the traveling family band.
4. Sacks and Sacks, "Way Up North in Dixie," 413. Bones were often called "bone castanets," or just "castanets."
5. A letter cited by Sacks and Sacks asks the Snowdens to "copy the song of the old Kentucky Home for me." "Way Up North in Dixie," 413.
6. See Sacks and Sacks, "Way Up North in Dixie," or their book of the same title for much more on this connection between the Snowdens and Emmett.
7. Nathan, *Dan Emmett*, 109. In James Kendall's *Clarinet Instruction Book*, from 1845, a "Negro Jig" is attributed the "Old Dan Emmit," which is a different tune than "Snowden's Jig." Rather than adapting a Black source, however, Emmett could have been writing songs in imitation of Black music. Dan Emmett said that he wrote his "first negro song" for Frank Whitaker, a "negro singer"— meaning, not that Whitaker was Black, but that he was a Blackface Minstrel performer. The 1870 census lists Frank Whitaker as a white man, and he was a circus performer in the 1860s and 1870s.
8. Sacks and Sacks, "Way Up North in Dixie," 425.

BIBLIOGRAPHY

Abrahams, Roger D. *Singing the Master: The Emergence of African American Culture in the Plantation South*. New York: Pantheon Books, 1992.

Agawu, Kofi. "Structural Analysis or Cultural Analysis? Competing Perspectives on the 'Standard Pattern' of West African Rhythm." *Journal of the American Musicological Society* 59, no. 1 (2006): 1–46.

Allen, William Francis, Charles Pickard Ware, and Lucy McKim Garrison. *Slave Songs of the United States*. New York: A. Simpson, 1867.

Beckford, William. *A Descriptive Account of the Island of Jamaica*. Vol. 2. London: T. and J. Egerton, 1790.

Bowdich, Thomas Edward. *Mission from Cape Coast Castle to Ashantee*. London: John Murray, 1819.

Briggs, Thomas F. *Briggs' Banjo Instructor*. Boston: Oliver Ditson, 1855.

Brown, Vincent. *Tacky's Revolt: The Story of an Atlantic Slave War*. Cambridge, MA: Harvard University Press, 2022.

Browne, Randy M. "*Surviving Slavery: Politics, Power, and Authority in the British Caribbean, 1807–1834*." PhD diss., University of North Carolina at Chapel Hill, 2012.

Burnard, Trevor. *Mastery, Tyranny, and Desire: Thomas Thistlewood and His Slaves in the Anglo-Jamaican World*. Chapel Hill: University of North Carolina Press, 2004.

Cairo, Aminata. "Hebi Sani: Mental Well Being Among the Working Class Afro-Surinamese in Paramaribo, Suriname." PhD diss., University of Kentucky, 2007.

Carlander, Christopher. *Dr. Christopher Carlanders resejournal, 1787–1788*. Edited by Christer Wijkström. Stockholm: Kungliga Vetenskapsakademien, 1979.

Charters, Samuel. *Songs of Sorrow: Lucy McKim Garrison and Slave Songs of the United States*. Jackson: University Press of Mississippi, 2015.

Chattleton, Kyle. "Music and Monticello's Enslaved Community." Monticello, March 12, 2021. www.monticello.org/exhibits-events/blog/music-and-monticello-s-enslaved-community.

Chernoff, John M. "The Rhythmic Medium in African Music." *New Literary History* 22, no. 4 (1991): 1093–102.

A Concise Historical Account of All the British Colonies in North-America, Comprehending Their Rise, Progress, and Modern State. London: J. Bew, 1775.

Converse, Frank B. "Banjo Reminiscences II." *Cadenza* 7, no. 11 (1901). https://archive.org/details/conversereminiscences/mode/1up.

Cresswell, Nicholas. *The Journal of Nicholas Cresswell, 1774–1777*. New York: Dial, 1924.

Dalton, Jim. "The Changing Intonational Practice of Mid-Nineteenth-Century Banjo." In *Banjo Roots and Branches*, edited by Robert B. Winans. Urbana: University of Illinois Press, 2018.

Davis, John. *Travels of John Davis in the United States of America, 1798 to 1802*. Edited by John Vance Cheney. Boston: Bibliophile Society, 1910.

de Bercy, Drouin. *De Saint-Domingue : de ses guerres, de ses révolutions, de ses ressources, et des moyens à prendre pour y rétablir la paix et l'industrie*. Paris: Hocquet, 1814.

Desch-Obi, T. J. "Combat and the Crossing of the *Kalunga*." In *Central Africans and Cultural Transformations in the American Diaspora*, edited by Linda M. Heywood. Cambridge. Cambridge University Press, 2009.

Dewulf, Jeroen. *The Pinkster King and the King of the Kongo: The Forgotten History of America's*

Dutch-Owned Slaves. Jackson: University Press of Mississippi, 2017.

Dewulf, Jeroen. "Rediscovering a Hudson Valley Folkloric Tradition: Traces of the 'Pinkster' Feast in Forgotten Books." *Hudson River Valley Review* 34, no. 2 (2018): 2–20.

Dickson, William. *Letters on Slavery*. London: J. Phillips, 1789.

Dickson, William. *Mitigation of Slavery*. London: LLD, 1814.

DjeDje, Jacqueline Cogdell. "Song Type and Performance Style in Hausa and Dagomba Possession (Bori) Music." *Black Perspective in Music* 12, no. 2 (1984): 166–82.

Douglass, Frederick. *Narrative of the Life of Frederick Douglass, an American Slave, Written by Himself.* Boston: Anti-Slavery Society, 1845.

Dubois, Laurent. *Avengers of the New World: The Story of the Haitian Revolution*. Cambridge, MA: Harvard University Press, 2009.

Dubois, Laurent. *The Banjo: America's African Instrument*. Cambridge, MA: Belknap Press of Harvard University Press, 2016.

Edwards, Bryan. *The History, Civil and Commercial, of the British Colonies in the West Indies in Two Volumes*. Dublin: Luke White, 1793.

Epstein, Dena. *Sinful Tunes and Spirituals: Black Music before the Civil War*. Urbana: University of Illinois Press, 1977.

Fermin, Philip. *Nieuwe algemeene beschryving van de colonie van Suriname* [. . .]. Harlingen: Van der Plaats junior, 1770.

Fernández Olmos, Margarite, and Lizabeth Paravisini-Gebert. *Creole Religions of the Caribbean: An Introduction from Vodou and Santeria to Obeah and Espiritismo*. New York: New York University Press, 2003.

Flint, Timothy. *Recollections of the Last Ten Years*. Boston: Cummings, Hilliard, 1826.

Floyd, Samuel A., Jr. "Black Music in the Cirum-Caribbean." *American Music* 17, no. 1 (1999): 1–38.

Focke, H. C. "Banja." In *Neger-Engelsch woordenboek*. Leiden: P. H. van den Heuvell, 1855.

Focke, H. C. "De Surinaamische negermuzijk." In *West-Indië: Bijdragen tot de bevordering van de kennis der Nederlandsch West-Indische koloniën*, vol. 2, edited by A. C. Kruseman. Haarlem: A. C. Kruseman, 1858.

Franklin, Maria. *Early Black Spirituality and the Cultural Strategy of Protective Symbolism: Evidence from Art and Archaeology*. Williamsburg, VA: Colonial Williamsburg Foundation, Department of Archaeological Research, 1997.

Gaddy, Kristina R. "The Banjo before Stringbands." Presentation, Stringband Summit, East Tennessee State University, Johnson City, February 10, 2023.

Gaddy, Kristina R. *Well of Souls: Uncovering the Banjo's Hidden History*. New York: W. W. Norton, 2022.

Garrison Family Papers. Sophia Smith Collection of Women's History, Smith College, Northampton, MA.

Geggus, David. "Haitian Voodoo in the Eighteenth Century: Language, Culture, Resistance." *Jahrbuch für Geschichte Lateinamerikas* 28, no. 1 (1991): 21–52.

Gerlach, Don R. "Black Arson in Albany, New York: November 1793." *Journal of Black Studies* 7, no. 3 (1977): 301–12.

Gerstin, Julian. "Tangled Roots: Kalenda and Other Neo-African Dances in the Circum-Caribbean." *New West Indian Guide* 78, no. 1–2 (2004): 5–41.

Gipson, Jennifer. "'A Strange, Ventriloquous Voice': Louisiana Creole, Whiteness, and the Racial Politics of Writing Orality." *Journal of American Folklore* 129, no. 514 (2016): 459–85.

Green, Edward C. "Winti and Christianity: A Study in Religious Change." *Ethnohistory* 25, no. 3 (1978): 251–76.

Guda, Trudi. "Banya: A Surviving Surinamese Slave Play." In *English- and Dutch-Speaking Regions*, vol. 2 of *A History of Literature in the Caribbean*, edited by A. James Arnold. Philadelphia: John Benjamins, 2001.

Halpert, Herbert. 1939 Southern States Recording Expedition (AFC 1939/005), Library of Congress, American Folklife Collection.

Handler, Jerome S., and Kenneth M. Bilby. "On the Early Use and Origin of the Term 'Obeah' in Barbados and the Anglophone Caribbean." *Slavery & Abolition* 22, no. 2 (2001): 87–100.

Handler, Jerome S., and Charlotte J. Frisbie. "Aspects of Slave Life in Barbados: Music and Its Cultural Context." *Caribbean Studies* 11, no. 4 (1972): 5–46.

Herskovits, Melville J., and Frances S. Herskovits. *Suriname Folk-Lore*. New York: AMS Press, 1936.

Heywood, Linda M., and John K. Thornton. *Central Africans, Atlantic Creoles, and the Foundation of the Americas, 1585–1660*. Cambridge: Cambridge University Press, 2007.

Holmes, Isaac. *An Account of the United States of America, Derived from Actual Observation, during a Residence of Four Years in That Republic: Including Original Communications*. London: Caxton, 1823.

Hubard Family Papers. University of North Carolina Southern Folklife Collection, Wilson Library, University of North Carolina at Chapel Hill.

Hungerford, James. *The Old Plantation, and What I Gathered There in an Autumn Month*. New York: Harper and Brothers, 1859.

Jefferson, Thomas. *Notes on the State of Virginia*. Paris, 1785. Boston: Lily and Wait, 1832.

Keller, Robert M., Raoul F. Camus, Kate Van Winkle Keller, and Susan Cifaldi. *Early American Secular Music and Its European Sources, 1589–1839: An Index*. Annapolis, MD: Colonial Music Institute, 2002. www.cdss.org/elibrary/Easmes/index.html.

Labat, Jean-Baptiste. *Nouveau voyage aux isles de l'Amérique*. Vol. 1. Paris: Guillaume Cavalier, 1722.

Leigh, Devin. "The Jamaican Airs: An Introduction to Unpublished Pieces of Musical Notation from Enslaved People in the Eighteenth-Century Caribbean." *Atlantic Studies* 17, no. 4 (2020): 462–84.

Leigh, Devin. "The Jamaican Airs Exhibit." *Early Caribbean Digital Archive*, Northeastern University, 2019. ecda.northeastern.edu/Jamaican-music-exhibit-leigh.

Leslie, Paul. *Low Country Shamanism: An Exploration of the Magical and Healing Practices of the Coastal Carolinas and Georgia*. N.p.: Path Notes Press, 2014.

Lichtveld, Ursy M., and Jan Voorhoeve, eds., *Creole Drum: An Anthology of Creole Literature in Suriname*. New Haven, CT: Yale University Press, 1975.

Lingold, Mary Caton. *African Musicians in the Atlantic World*. Charlottesville: University of Virginia Press, 2023.

Lingold, Mary Caton, Laurent Dubois, and David Garner. *Musical Passage*. Accessed August 8, 2024. www.musicalpassage.org.

Lomax, John A. Southern States Collection (AFC 1935/002), Library of Congress, American Folklife Collection.

Lowery, I. M. *Life on the Old Plantation in the Ante-Bellum Days*. Columbia, SC: State Co. Printers, 1911.

Luffman, John. *A Brief Account of the Island of Antigua*. London: J. Luffman, 1790.

McKim Garrison, Lucy. "Songs of the Port Royal 'Contrabands.'" *Dwight's Journal of Music* 21, no. 6 (1862): 254–55.

Métraux, Alfred. *Voodoo in Haiti*. Translated by Hugo Chateris. New York: Schocken Books, 1972.

Nadeau, Roland. "The Grace and Beauty of Classic Rags: Structural Elements in a Distinct Musical Genre." In *Ragtime: Its History, Composers, and Music*, edited by John Edward Hasse. New York: Schirmer, 1985.

Nathan, Hans. *Dan Emmett and the Rise of Early Negro Minstrelsy*. Norman: University of Oklahoma Press, 1977.

Njoku, Chijioke. "Idioms of Religion, Music, Dance, and African Art Forms." In *West African Masking Traditions and Diaspora Masquerade Carnivals: History, Memory, and Transnationalism*. Rochester, NY: University of Rochester Press, 2020.

Northrup, Solomon. *Twelve Years a Slave*. 1853; repr. New York: Dover, 1970.

Pendlebury, Celia. "Tune Families and Tune Histories: Melodic Resemblances in British and Irish Folk Tunes." *Folk Music Journal* 11, no. 5 (2020): 67–95.

Pettinger, Alasdair. "'Eh! Eh! Bomba, Hen! Hen!' Making Sense of a Vodou Chant." In *Obeah and Other Powers*, edited by Diana Paton and Maarit Forde. Durham, NC: Duke University Press, 2012.

Pinckard, George. *Notes on the West Indies*. London: Baldwin, Cradock, and Joy, 1816.

Pinn, Anthony B. *Varieties of African American Religious Experience*. Minneapolis, MN: Fortress, 1997.

Prest, Julia. "Pale Imitations: White Performances of Slave Dance in the Public Theatres of Pre-Revolutionary Saint-Domingue." *Atlantic Studies* 16, no. 4 (2019): 502–20.

Raboteau, Albert J. *Slave Religion: The "Invisible Institution" in the Antebellum South*. New York: Oxford University Press, 1980.

Rath, Richard Cullen. "African Music in Seventeenth-Century Jamaica: Cultural Transit and Transition." *William and Mary Quarterly*, 3rd ser., 50, no. 4 (1993): 700–726.

Robertson, Wyndham. *Pocahontas, Alias Matoaka, and Her Descendants through Her Marriage at Jamestown, Virginia, in April, 1614, with John Rolfe, Gentleman*. Richmond, VA: J. W. Randolph and English, 1887.

Ross, Pete. Interview with Kristina R. Gaddy, April 22, 2024.

Sacks, Howard L., and Judith R. Sacks. *Way Up North in Dixie: A Black Family's Claim to the Confederate Anthem*. Washington, DC: Smithsonian Institution Press, 1993.

Sacks, Howard L., and Judith R. Sacks. "Way Up North in Dixie: Black-White Musical Interaction in Knox County, Ohio." *American Music* 6, no. 4 (1988): 409–27.

Saltator. *A Treatise on Dancing and Various Other Matters* [. . .]. Boston: Commercial Gazette, 1802.

Schöpf, Johann David. *Travels in the Confederation, 1783–1784: From the German of Johann David Schoepf.* Translated by Alfred James Morrison. New York: Bergman, 1968.

Schreyer, Lowell. "The Banjo in Ragtime." In *Ragtime: Its History, Composers, and Music*, edited by John Edward Hasse. New York: Schirmer, 1985.

Schuler, Monica. *Alas, Alas, Kongo*. Baltimore: Johns Hopkins University Press, 1980.

Sharp, Cecil J. *English Folk-Chanteys*. New York: H. W. Gray, 1914.

Sloane, Hans. *A Voyage to the Islands Madera, Barbados, Nieves, S. Christophers and Jamaica, . . . In Large Copper Plates as Big as the Life*. Vol. 1. London: B. M., 1707.

Stedman, John Gabriel. *Stedman's Suriname: Life in an Eighteenth-Century Slave Society; An Abridged, Modernized Edition of Narrative of a Five Years' Expedition against the Revolted Negroes of Surinam*. Edited by Richard and Sally Price. Baltimore: Johns Hopkins University Press, 1992.

Taylor, John. *Jamaica in 1687: The Taylor Manuscript at the National Library of Jamaica*. Edited by David Buisseret. Kingston, Jamaica: University of the West Indies Press, 2008.

Terry, R. R. "Sea Songs and Shanties." *Proceedings of the Musical Association*, 41st Sess. (1914–15): 135–40.

Thistlewood, Thomas, Papers. James Marshall and Marie-Louise Osborn Collection, Beinecke Rare Book and Manuscript Library, Yale University, New Haven, CT.

Thomasson, Fredrik. *Svarta St. Barthelemy: Människoöden i en svensk koloni, 1785–1847*. Stockholm: Natur & Kultur, 2022.

Thompson, Robert Farris. *Flash of the Spirit: African and Afro-American Art and Philosophy*. New York: Random House, 1983.

Thornton, John K. "African Dimensions of the Stono Rebellion." *American Historical Review* 94, no. 4 (1991): 1101–13.

Thornton, John K. "Religious and Ceremonial Life in the Kongo and Mbundu Areas, 1500–1700." In *Central Africans and Cultural Transformations in the American Diaspora*, edited by Linda Haywood. Cambridge: Cambridge University Press, 2002.

Tucker, George. *The Valley of Shenandoah; or, Memoirs of the Graysons*. Chapel Hill: University of North Carolina Press, 1970.

University of North Carolina Papers. University Archives, Wilson Library, University of North Carolina at Chapel Hill.

Wells, Paul F. "Fiddling as an Avenue of Black-White Musical Interchange." *Black Music Research Journal* 23, no. 1–2 (2003): 135–47.

Whisnant, David. *All That Is Native and Fine*. Chapel Hill: University of North Carolina Press, 1983.

Williams, Cynric. *A Tour through the Island of Jamaica: From the Western to the Eastern End in the Year 1823*. London: Hunt and Clarke, 1826.

Winans, Robert B. "Black Musicians in Eighteenth-Century America: Evidence from Runaway Slave Advertisements." In *Banjo Roots and Branches*, edited by Robert B. Winans. Urbana: University of Illinois Press, 2018.

Winslow, David J. "A Negro Corn-Shucking." *Journal of American Folklore* 86, no. 339 (1973): 61–62.

INDEX

Page numbers in italics refer to illustrations.

Note: "Haiti" is indexed under "Saint-Domingue" before the Haitian Revolution.